By JERRY YOUNG
WITH TED GUTHRIE

America's First
Observed Trials
Champion

IN COLLABORATION WITH
BOB WENTZEL

PAGE PUBLISHING, INC.
Conneaut Lake, PA

First originally published by Page Publishing 2021

ISBN 978-1-6624-1753-5 (pbk)
ISBN 978-1-6624-1754-2 (digital)

Printed in the United States of America

I first met Jerry Young at a Trials Inc. observed trials event in West Virginia. Together with my wife, Diane, and son, Quinn, we happened to be joined for breakfast one morning by Jerry, along with his son and daughter-in-law, Ryan and Adrianna. Jerry and I were seated directly across from one another, struck up a conversation, and soon found that in addition to motorcycles, we also had common business interests—specifically natural gas distribution. That initial conversation eventually led to a lasting friendship, which continues to this day.

In the course of meeting up with Jerry at subsequent trials events and other motorcycle-related activities, he shared with me fascinating stories of his various experiences over the years, and I found myself most intrigued by this man and all he has accomplished in his lifetime.

In time, the idea occurred to me that Jerry's story would make for a very interesting book. When I approached him with my thoughts on putting his stories together in book form, in typically modest fashion, Jerry was at first hesitant. However, after several more discussions on the subject, he agreed to give it a try.

Well, it's taken three years, and thanks to the hours and hours of work put in by Ted Guthrie to research and assemble an extensive amount of material and then actually put Jerry's thoughts and words to paper, it finally all came together. Hope you enjoy it.

—Bob Wentzel

Among the many things I love about Jerry is his never-ending zest for adventure. I was ferrying him somewhere on my KTM Adventurer one day and happened to catch his big grin in the bike's mirror. The image was too precious to pass up, so I grabbed a photo. I believe it captures Jerry's entire outlook on motorcycling, and on life.

—Bob Wentzel

CONTENTS

ACKNOWLEDGMENTS

First and foremost, I wish to thank my good friend, Bob Wentzel, who first introduced to me the idea of doing a book about my life and times. This came as quite a surprise to me as up to that point, I could not have imagined that there was sufficient interest, by anyone, for a book about Jerry Young. And yet with Bob's support and encouragement, here we are.

I also wish to thank my lovely wife, Kelly, without whose support the opportunities for all that I have experienced over the years would not have been possible. And to each of my children, I love each and every one of you deeply and very much hope your lives have been favorably influenced by our various experiences together.

Thanks also to those individuals who contributed to the content of this book, such as Jim Ellis, Ashley Foy, especially Ted Guthrie, who spent three years writing this book so that my story could be shared. I very much appreciate the efforts you all put forth to see this project through to completion.

And I must express a tremendous thank you to all my friends and associates, both within and outside of the motorcycling community. It is your friendship, and our experiences together, which have greatly enriched my life. I appreciate you all more than I could ever express.

INTRODUCTION

Yes, it's true. Before Bernie Schreiber, Marland Whaley, Lane Levitt, and all the other National Observed Trials Champions—all the guys you saw pictures of and read about in magazines—a totally unknown rider, new to the sport, won the very first AMA National Observed Trials Championship.

And this rider was no youngster either, winning the title at thirty-one years of age. Further, he was not part of any team or riding out of a shop. In fact, at the time, he had no sponsorship whatsoever. He was just an average working man with a wife and kids and had to be back on the job every Monday morning, regardless of where his travels took him in pursuit of the championship. But what's most amazing is that this rider competed and won, aboard not a purpose-built, factory-designed observed trials motorcycle but rather a modified 1967 Triumph Mountain Cub—just a little four-stroke street bike which the Triumph factory fitted out with provisions for mild trail riding.

All this adds up to the amazing story of an exceptionally skilled, talented, dedicated individual who, throughout his lifetime, has accomplished so much. This, then, is the story of Jerry Young, America's first Observed Trials Champion.

CHAPTER I
Biography

Who I Am, Where I've Been, What I've Done

I was born in 1940 in Williamsport, Pennsylvania. Central part of the state. Beautiful country. Not many motorcycles around though as I remember. Oh, certainly there had to have been some prewar Harleys and Indians and who-knows-what-else plying about, but mine was certainly not a "motorcycling family," that's for sure.

Dad was a design engineer, a draftsman, with the Darling Valve & Manufacturing Company, there in Williamsport. As was typical of the era, my mother was a "stay-at-home" mom. In fact, it was not until age sixty-five and due to a family circumstance that she learned to drive, obtained a driver's license, and took a job.

This is a favorite picture of my mom and dad, taken when they were first together. I am most intrigued by the string running from dad's fingers—apparently some sort of means he had rigged up to trip the camera's shutter remotely. A very early "selfie"!

So, in 1940, the US was just getting over the Great Depression and was about to enter into a world war. Opportunities were out there, but you had to work for them. I started going to work with my dad on weekends when I was still just a kid and learned the craft of wood patternmaking. That was pretty cool as it involved working from blueprints to create, in wood, a mold, which would eventually be used to produce metal products.

Many folks back then were very self-sufficient, did everything themselves, and rarely hired outside help. My dad, for example, built our house all by himself. I helped with every aspect of the construction and, in turn, learned all the skills involved, such as carpentry, masonry, electrical, plumbing, etc. Dad was a great mentor in many ways and a great teacher, very skilled in virtually all trades. He was also a thirty-second-degree Mason. That title may not mean much to most folks these days, but look it up and you'll see just what an accomplishment that was for my father.

I did not do all that well in school. In fact, I flunked both the third and fourth grades. I didn't know it at the time and am unsure if the condition was even recognized back then, but it turns out that I suffer from dyslexia. That, of course, made reading very difficult for me. It wasn't until years later that, with the help of improved learning techniques, I was able to overcome much of what held me back in school.

I grew up with two siblings, an older brother and sister. Mom played the piano and loved art and flower arranging. Ours was a home always filled with art and music. My brother, Nick, studied auto mechanics. Working along with him, I learned the basics as well. Nick later took up oil painting and went on to study art in New York City. Sister Yvonne was intent on moving above and beyond little old Williamsport. She first studied modeling in Cincinnati, Ohio, and then in New York City. Eventually, she went on to actually work as a model. It was in New York City that she met her husband, and they both ended up doing very well for themselves. Yvonne became a successful author and playwright, with articles regularly featured in *The New York Times* and had several cookbooks published by Random House. She and her husband were also quite the amateur magicians.

There were some unique opportunities provided me through my sister's success. After graduating high school, I was working in a pattern shop. When laid off, on occasion, I would travel to New York City to stay with my sister and brother-in-law. While there, I performed carpentry work and other remodeling on their elegant home. I also spent a month in Jamaica with my sister and her family during their vacation there on the island, serving as babysitter for Yvonne's two young children. Let me tell you, those were real eye-opening experiences for a young kid from Pennsylvania.

Throughout my childhood and teen years, there were still no motorcycles, however. My hobbies, then, included archery. I got a hickory recurve bow, which I still own. Got pretty good at it too. I'd set up bottle caps for targets, and from 20 yards out, I could get two to three arrows into each cap. I began competing, and even while still just a little kid would square off against adults, shooting up to 80 yards to the target—and that's with no sights! Hey, about the arrows I used, my weekly allowance was just twenty-five cents, and arrows were expensive! So, I'd make up what we called "flu-flu" arrows, which had feathers all around the shaft to slow them down, made it easier to locate and retrieve the arrows when the target was overshot. I also enjoyed aquariums and fish, still do. Picked up on that hobby in school, as we had an aquarium in the classroom, where I was honored with the awesome responsibility of feeding the fish.

This is how it was. Skills developed through hours of practice with my old recurve bow helped later in my life to at times put food on the table. Check that cool hat.

Eventually, I got myself a car. By then, it was the late '50s, and the hot rod and customizing scene was in full swing. I had a 1950 Ford convertible. Performed all kinds of metal work on it. Remember, these were the "lead sled" days. Guys were filling and forming every whichway, working to make their rides unique from any other. I'd been working on learning to become a welder and put these talents to good use on the Ford because back then, we did all the custom work in metal—welding, brazing, and leading. I eventually installed a '53 Mercury engine in my car, which boosted the power a bit from its original flat head. I also installed an Edelbrock intake, set up to accept two two-barrel carbs. My main competition while out street racing was 1950s Oldsmobiles. They had the hot factory engines and were the cars to beat. I did okay but kept breaking transmissions. Most Fords like mine were equipped with three-speed manual transmissions, "three on the tree," baby! I honestly remember going through twenty-three manual transmissions before switching over to an automatic, which interestingly held up. Go figure.

Had my share of girlfriends, including some nice ladies I met while spending time at my sister's place in New York City. Eventually, I met and married a hometown girl. My first wife, Carlene, and I were married in 1961. We had four kids together—Todd, Laura Lee, Mike, and Ryan. Sadly, the marriage did not last. We divorced, but I eventually met and married my current wife, Kelley. We've been together since 1981. Together, we have three children—Kaitlyn, Sairin, and Chessa.

So, yes, I've got a big family. As such, the associated expenses in raising that many kids has had a lot to do with dictating the need for creative means of pursuing my motorcycling hobby. I've always been just an average, hardworking guy. No fancy, high-end positions for me. One of my first jobs was with a pattern shop. Problem was I kept getting laid off. With a wife and kids to support, there were times when it required me to go out and hunt in order to put food on the table. I also resorted to going on welfare—just once for about six months. That government assistance paid us $40.00 per week. And guess what? I had to pay it back! That's right. Back then, Federal assistance was just a "loan" to help individuals and families get back on their feet. Once gainful employment was reestablished, the money had to be repaid. My, how times have changed.

My high school yearbook photo. How about that slicked-down hairdo?

I later went on to work at a furniture factory making desks. Then I worked at the local Chrysler-Plymouth dealer as a "grease monkey." Don't know if that was an official title, but that's what they called guys like me whose job it was to do oil changes and to chase parts. That job paid all of $2.25 per hour. I aspired, however, to become a full-fledged mechanic, a position which paid two dollars and thirty-five cents per hour, wow! Those were pretty mundane jobs, none of which obviously paid much money.

Good fortune finally shone my way, however. I was throwing darts a few nights a week, and one of the guys I got to know was superintendent at the local gas company. This guy's name was Clarence Golf, who we all called "Gooch." Clarence offered me a job digging ditches, which in turn led to a better position within the company, fixing regulators. I proved myself with them through plain old hard work and ambition, eventually becoming foreman of the Regulator Department. It was with this company—Scranton Springbrook Water Company, later Pennsylvania Gas & Water, then PG Energy and currently known as UGI Utilities (whew!)—that I worked the balance of my career. It was good work with an excellent company, for which I owe considerable gratitude to my old buddy, Gooch.

As the result of finally establishing myself with a good company and working steadily at decent wages, I was able to purchase some land and, with the assistance of my father, built my first and only house. The wife and kids and I had been living in a mobile home, but once we'd put enough money aside, I made arrangements to purchase a "Lundy" home. This was quite an arrangement as the Lundy people constructed complete walls at their facility then trucked them to the jobsite. At that point, it was just a matter of erecting the walls and connecting everything together. However, I first had to hire a con-tractor to dig the basement. Next, I arranged for a friend to do the block work, but when he didn't show up, I took on the job myself. I'd done some masonry work in the past, and having watched my friend do some of it, I finished up the foundation. Framework, carpentry, plumbing, electrical, I did it all. That was in 1967. Between the land, construction of the house, all materials, well, and septic, we had a total of $12,700 invested in the place. Hard to believe. And I must have done it all pretty well because we're still living there and the place hasn't fallen apart yet.

So, that's a little bit about what makes me, me! And with that said, let's get on to the motorcycle stuff.

CHAPTER 2

Enter the Cub

"The little bike that could."

So, it's the late 1960s, and at this point in my life, I had not yet even ridden a motorcycle. But then one day, I was in town, and a friend came by on his 650 Triumph Bonneville. He stopped to talk, and I asked if I could take a ride on the bike. "Sure!" he said. So, off I went. Remember, no experience whatsoever, but hell, I was full of piss and vinegar and figured I could handle anything.

All went well until I came to a stoplight, and that's when things got a bit complicated. There was a light rain falling, and as I attempted to get stopped, I suddenly remembered my friend's reminder that the Triumph would not idle. So, clutch in, feathering the throttle, intersection getting closer and closer, wet, slippery conditions; in the end, I ended up applying a bit too much rear brake. The Triumph promptly low-sided, and bike and rider both slid right out into the middle of the intersection. No cross traffic fortunately, and with the bike on its side but still running, I pulled in the clutch, stood it back up, and continued on like nothing had happened. On my way back, and undaunted by the misfortune back at the intersection, I wicked it up and passed by where my friend was waiting, doing about 90 mph, or so it felt. And all this, in the rain, no helmet, and no experience. Oh, the things we've gotten away with!

All right, so now I've got motorcycles on my mind, and soon after, I went to an automobile and motorcycle show in New York City while visiting with my sister and brother-in-law. This was in the spring of 1968, and I came home intent on purchasing my own bike. A big British twin was what I had in mind, but funds were tight, and one of the few used bikes in my price range which caught my eye was a one-year-old 1967 Triumph Mountain Cub. Just 200cc though.

Nothing like what I thought I needed. But I went to look at the bike anyway and actually liked what I saw. Nice-looking little bike, and I couldn't find a thing wrong with it. A couple of test rides showed the Cub had acceptable power and was quite comfortable. So, I decided to go for it and struck a deal. The bike had 550 miles on it, and I got it for $550.

And it worked out great! I rode the Cub all over the place that summer, as did my wife. I'd be out riding, come home, the wife would jump right on the bike, and take off. Together, we put 5,000 road miles on the little 200 in the first year we owned it.

The Cub as it looked when I first got it. Picture was taken in my front yard. Just playing around a bit and doing some wheelies.

One thing to remember about the old Cub is that it was definitely a "family" bike. In addition to myself and my wife, as soon as they got old enough, our kids rode the heck out of that little motorcycle. From back to front: Mike, Laura Lee, and Todd.

In addition to riding on the road, I was also doing some trail riding with a friend of mine who owned a Bultaco Matador. One thing led to another, and soon this fellow invited me to participate with him in the Burro Enduro, which was held in Chemung, New York. I had never before ridden an enduro, or any other competition event for that matter, and was not one to go off half-cocked. So, I got a copy of Bud Ekins' book *How to Ride and Win*, studied up on enduro riding and timekeeping, and that was the extent of my preparation. As for the Cub, I installed a number plate over top of the headlight and mounted up a route chart holder. Other than that, the bike was as from the factory.

So, we get out there, and once my number came up, I took off, headed down the trail, and wouldn't you know I zeroed the first check! Thought to myself at that point, *This enduro riding is a piece of cake.* And then I came to a hill. Wow, there were riders stuck all over it. I surveyed the situation for a while and then decided to go for it. The Cub didn't have much power, but sometimes that can work to your advantage. Rather than spinning the rear wheel, we just motored right on up that hill. At one point, I ran over another rider's front wheel but just kept on going. There were people standing at the top, and as soon I got close, a couple of guys grabbed the front wheel and pulled me right over. There was a check up there, and once again, I thought I had this whole enduro thing figured out.

Off I went again, but then I got lost, wandered around looking for arrows for a while, and when I finally found some and started following them, I thought, *Uh-oh, these trails look familiar.* Sure enough, next thing I know, I was right back down at the bottom of that same hill. I was pretty tired and frustrated at this point and sure didn't feel like tackling that hill again, so I decided to call it a day. I got some directions on how to ride out of the woods other than by way of the hill and so went back to the clubhouse. Despite missing several checks as a result, and much to my surprise, when the awards were handed out, I was called up there for first in the Lightweight Class! Evidently, the other riders in that class had an even more difficult time than I did. And that was my first trophy, a first place, in my first competition event. Some start!

On the way home from the Burro, my Matador-riding friend told me that he was going to a place called Candytown the next week to ride an observed trials event and asked if I wanted to go along and compete. I had never even heard of observed trials, but with that first-place trophy in my hand, I was feeling just all full of myself. Figured there was nothing my little Cub and I couldn't handle, so I said, "Count me in!"

This is how it all began. I had just gotten home from my first Enduro, and was showing off my very first trophy. Total modifications to the Cub at this point consisted of a number plate over the headlight, and a fire extinguisher(!) bolted to the frame. Note the oem, trials-universal tires. Hadn't even mounted up knobbies, yet.

So, the next week, we headed out to Candytown. And, no, that's not the name of a town, it's simply what this riding area is called due to its proximity to Hershey, Pennsylvania, you know, where the Hershey candy factory is located. Makes sense now, right? Anyway, with some coaching from my friend, I headed out onto the course and started riding sections. Remember, at this point, the Cub was still stone-stock, as from the factory—lights, stock gearing, street tires, and the whole deal. But despite those handicaps, I came away that day with a fourth place in the Novice Class. And I went back two weeks later and got first place in the Novice Class! I was beginning to like this trials stuff.

This picture shows what it was really like in the early days of Trials. No helmet, no riding gear, and check out the Cub: Stripped down and modified, yet I hadn't even removed the headlight mounting arms at this point. Given the height I've got the front end elevated here, there must have been quite some obstacle—likely a big rock, just in front of me.

Over the next several years, I continued to compete on the Cub in enduros, hare scrambles, and observed trials. One of the best enduro events I participated in on the little bike was the 1971 Berkshire International Two-Day Trials. This, of course, was the classic Berkshire event held in Pittsfield, Massachusetts. It was a great experience. All the top riders were there, and I was very excited to be a part of it. The trails were awesome, and despite some rain on Saturday, riding conditions were pretty good. The bike developed a bit of a miss in it as the day unfolded but kept on running. We put in 180 miles that day. Then it poured down rain all night. Sunday started well; as despite sitting outside in impound through that hard rain, the little Cub fired right up. The rain had made things really sloppy though. Slowed me down quite a bit. I made it to 300 miles before houring out, and since that meant my score was a DNF, I wrapped it up. Even so, the final results had me listed at 151st position out of 300 starters. It was a grueling event to be sure, but thinking back on it now, wow! All those miles, in pretty nasty conditions, and on such a modest little bike. Guess we just didn't know any better!

Now, throughout all this, the Cub remained my one and only motorcycle. In addition to competition, I still rode it on the street, went trail riding all the time, and used it for some utility work as well. Case in point, I once hauled a deer out of the woods on the bike. Yep, during hunting season one year, I had bagged my deer. Dragged it to a point where I could ride out on the Cub, slung the deer over the gas tank, climbed aboard, and with the deer in lap started back up a steep cow pasture toward home. The deer's head was hanging down on the spark plug side of the bike and eventually started dripping blood right on the plug cap. There was evidently sufficient conductivity involved to transfer juice from the plug, through the deer, and into me—right where the deer's body was making contact—in my lap. End result was getting zapped pretty strongly right in the groin! That's one experience I don't care to repeat.

It was later in '71 that I decided to move away from riding enduros and focus on observed trials competition and subsequently made the decision to begin modifying the Cub accordingly. There were, of course, other machines on the market by this time which were designed and built by the factories specifically for trials riding. However, the Cub simply worked so darn well for me that I figured I could make it even better rather than trading out to a different bike.

Even though this was still early in my modification efforts, you can see how much has already been done to the Cub. Stripped down of course, altered top tube increased ground clearance, under-seat tank, 21" front wheel, Ceriani forks, and a Mikuni carb, just to name a few of the changes I had incorporated.

First step was some pretty obvious stuff—I removed all and any parts no longer required, such as lighting equipment and the factory tank and seat. Ground clearance had always been an issue, so I switched out the stock 19-inch front wheel for a 21-inch. Rear wheel was left alone save for mounting up a wider rear tire, 4-inch in place of the factory 3.50-incher. This all sounds like small potatoes these days, but remember, Cubs were little, very rudimentary bikes, with origins going back to just after WWII! There was room for plenty of improvements, and I just let logic dictate what could, and should, be done to make the Cub into a more effective trials bike.

For example, the Triumph Cub's frame is a bit unique. If you've never seen a stock one with the tank removed, the top tube does not run back from near the stop of the steering head like on most bikes. Instead, it goes in a horizontal line starting several inches down the front frame down tube. I reconfigured all this by cutting and repositioning that top tube, plus the down tube, as well as altering the frame below and at the back of the engine. All this raised the engine

25

significantly, which was exactly what was needed to achieve additional ground clearance.

Remember, even my version of the Cub, the Mountain Cub, was not designed as a dirt bike but was rather just a little street bike with a few alterations. So, major improvements were called for. Oh, and throughout all this frame surgery, I brazed rather than welded each joint, just like Triumph did at the factory.

Next was to fab up something to replace the bike's big tank and seat. I first simply installed a little solo seat. That was easy. But for the fuel tank, I decided to make my own. I put a piece of two-inch metal pipe in my vice, rolled sheet metal around it, shaped it so it tapered from front to back, then welded up the seam. Flat stock capped both ends, with nice, secure weld joints there as well. For the filler opening, I welded in a one and one-quarter-inch nipple, topped with a threaded, cast-iron cap with a hole drilled in it for a vent. This all may sound a bit crude, and quite rudimentary, but remember that I was working at home, by myself, with simple materials I had on hand. And it all worked!

For those of you not aware, Triumph Cub engines are dry sump and so have a pretty good-size oil tank mounted remotely up under the seat. I chose to improve upon that factory tank and so welded one up out of sheet metal to be lighter and to tuck in better. I also rethought my fuel tank setup, which was still mounted in the factory location. With my new, smaller oil tank in place, there was some extra space left over under the seat. That gave me the idea to work up a fuel tank which, instead of being mounted up on the frame's top tube, could be moved down lower and double as a seat base. Lower center of gravity and all that. So, I fabbed one up, fitted it nicely into place, and, since trials is a "stand-up" sport, did away with a conventional seat entirely. Instead of any kind of typical seat or material, I just covered the top of the fuel tank/seat base with a piece of deer hide from that same deer I'd hauled out of the woods on the bike. Fur and all. Classy!

I've always believed that if riders can manage ice and snow-covered rocks, they can handle just about any conditions. Pennsylvania provided us with many such opportunities to challenge ourselves, accordingly.

Stock Triumph Cub forks are pretty rudimentary and clearly lacked the level of performance required for serious trials riding. I looked at other off-road bikes which were around at that time and, based on what I saw, decided to try a pair of Betor forks. I obtained a pair from a Bultaco and, along with the Bul's triple trees, and with some modifications to the steering stern and the fork stops on the Cub's frame, everything worked out quite nicely. While I was at it, I changed out the Cub's stock steering head ball bearings by welding in Bultaco conical races and fitted roller bearings. The Betors certainly functioned much better than the Cub's stock forks, but after some testing and evaluation, I eventually changed out the Betor lower tubes for Cerianis.

That took care of the front end of the bike. In the back, I lengthened the swing arm and fitted up a pair of Betor gas shocks. I also relocated the foot peg mounts and replaced the stockers with a pair of sturdy cleated pegs. The work I had done to alter the front of the frame had been an obvious need for improved ground clearance.

But you might wonder how I knew of a need to lengthen the swing-arm. Well, keep in mind that in this era, the '60s and '70s, there were a lot of modifications being performed to bikes, especially off-road bikes. Look through any bike magazine or two-wheel how-to book from the period and you'll find them loaded with features on serious modification instructions. The bikes from back then simply needed major mods to make them perform well. In my case, I lengthened the Cub's swingarm to help keep the front end down on uphill. In stock form, it simply wanted to loop out much too easily.

Taken at a very nice event put on by The Ohio Valley BSA Owners Club. Not many rocks to be seen in this particular image, but there are plenty of them at this venue. Decades of development work on the old Cub resulted in a level of performance which is quite effective in virtually all kinds of terrain. Note that just a touch of front brake is all that's needed, even on a steep downhill such as this one.

On to the motor. One of the reasons I held on to the Cub, performed all these modifications to it and kept riding and competing on the thing, is because it actually worked very well for me. That little 200cc four-stroke motor, although modest in power, really did get the job done. It was reliable too. Early Cub motors suffered from some design deficiencies, but by the time mine was produced, Triumph had developed the little motor about to the best it was ever going to be. There was, of course, always room for improvement. For my purposes, I really didn't need any more power, but in trials, power delivery is key. And so, in the interest of improved throttle response, I decided to try a Mikuni carburetor. Mounting one up was no easy task, however. I had to cut and weld the stock aluminum intake. Note that this effort, along with all my welding, was done with a torch. No stick or tig was available to me, so I worked with what I had. And anyone who knows anything about welding can attest to what a challenge it is to weld aluminum with a torch. But I got it done and am very pleased with the performance results. With effective tuning, the Mikuni worked out exactly as I had hoped and is still on the bike to this day. As far as the exhaust system, there wasn't any need for a radical change. The basic factory pipe and silencer have been retained, just slightly relocated, and with stronger mounts fabbed up.

You will note my reference in the last paragraph of "to this day." Yes, the Cub is still around and is in my possession. I never sold it, and I still ride and compete on the bike! Hey, it works and is really fun to ride. Plus, I've been tinkering with it and continually making improvements all these years. Have it looking pretty good these days, no more deer hide seat cover, for example. Ha-ha. Changes since those original modifications have in fact been mostly in the interest of refinement and cosmetics although many little things have been done to improve overall performance. For example, long ago, I worked with clutch pivot point, lever selection, and cable application to provide smooth, consistent, one-finger clutch operation. In regard to braking, the bike's original hubs are still in use. Careful matching of the shoes and hubs, plus effective lever-and-pivot-point setup has provided quite effective braking capability, and I can even quite easily perform front wheel stoppies.

The Cub never ceases to draw attention. A few years ago, my friend Bob Wentzel had invited me to participate in a Mid Atlantic Trials event in Ohio, and shortly after my arrival a fellow walked up and began asking questions about the Cub. Turns out it was Paul Danik, from Mars, Pennsylvania—ISDT gold medalist, who back in the 70's was part of John Penton's hand-picked team of riders. Paul went on to compete in multiple Six-Day Trials events.

Additionally, the Cub has survived absolute thrashing from all three of my sons. Each of them rode the bike at some point in time during their progression to larger, more modern machines.

My father even took a ride on the Cub, but just once. Without proper instruction, he took off and almost immediately had the throttle pinned wide open. Fortunately for both of us, I was in a position to intervene. As Dad passed by me, I actually grabbed him by the wrist and pulled him right off the bike! To say the little Cub has been through a lot is an understatement!

And so, it was on this machine that I got my start in motor-cycling, began what has now become a fifty-year-plus success in competition, and it was this bike which provided me with my first national championship. So, let's move on to what events led to my achieving the totally unexpected.

The Cub, along with my son, Ryan, and I, were at one point featured guests of the fine folks who make up Mid-Atlantic Ossa (http://www.maossa.com), at an event they hosted at the wonderful Broom Factory facility, in Baltimore, Maryland. Formerly an actual broom factory, this fine old building now provides space for various cultural displays and events. http://www.broomfactory.com. As part of the event, the Cub was set up for this fine, studio image.

CHAPTER 3

From Competitor
to Promoter

How I Went from Riding Local Trials to Hosting
National and International Trials Events

People have asked me how indeed I went from just a local guy riding
observed trials to not only hosting local trials events but also responsible for multiple national and international trials competitions. Well,
the "how" part, that's easy. Just plain, old hard work. The "why"?

A moment of quiet contemplation in my man cave, at a point when
I was about to take on more responsibilities and become involved
in more activities than I could ever imagined possible.

You see, when I first started riding trials, there were three places where I would typically go to compete, and interestingly enough, each featured somewhat different terrain and obstacles to challenge the riders. First was Candytown, which I would characterize as having "round rocks." Next is Lenheartsville, which was somewhat plain Jane, with sections involving a lot of climbing and descending of stream banks. And third, the White Rose M/C, a place with a lot of greasy, slippery clay soil and where we were always climbing over giant logs. And each of these places are a couple several hours drive from my home base. So, considering there was plenty of equally challenging and varied riding right around where I live, why not set up my own trials and, thus, have the other riders come to me? Seemed like a reasonably achievable goal. But there were a few things to first establish. For one thing, I had no club. Additionally, I needed to find somewhere to hold the events.

Okay. First things first. The AMA said that you need at least ten card-carrying AMA members to form a club. I approached ten riding buddies who were each AMA members, told them I was forming this club to host Trials events, and were they interested? I explained that I would do all the setup work—clear the loops and build the sections. All I really needed of them was to help out on the day of the event. So, I got my ten signatures, filed the paperwork, and there you go, I had a club. And that's how I formed the Pennsylvania Trials Riders, a.k.a. PTR. That was in 1969.

The PTR logo. Of all my life's accomplishments, establishment
and development of the Pennsylvania Trials Riders club
is among those of which I am most proud.

During this time, I was also checking out locations for us to host our events. The one I eventually settled upon is called Mackeyville and was at the time hosting old-time scrambles races. My buddy John Grove's brother-in-law owned the property, and through John, I soon formed an agreement to hold trials there to supplement their scrambles schedule. I liked this place in particular because it includes hills, a creek, and plenty of rocks. It lent itself quite well to our needs, and I knew we could put together some excellent trials events there.

Over the next few years, things went quite well. The PTR regularly hosted events, the riders enjoyed themselves and kept coming back, and through that plain, old hard work previously mentioned, we were a modest success. Now, by "success" I don't mean a lot of money. Instead of raking in a bunch of revenue, my intent on behalf of PTR was just to keep ourselves afloat and cover our operating costs, which were quite modest. We did a lot to keep costs down, even going so far as to make our own trophies. And our events were popular! We had riders coming in all the way from New England, specifically to ride PTR events.

So, all was well in the neighborhood, as the saying goes. Things were going so well in fact that I eventually got it in my head that, together with the PTR, we could host a national trials round.

Doing so, however, would not be as easy as simply getting set up to hold local District 6 AMA events. Fortunately for me, one of the riders who had been coming in from New England to ride our events, a fellow named Dave Russell, told Wiltz Wagner of the North American Trials Council about PTR and how this guy named Jerry Young was doing such a great job of putting on top-quality trials.

Dr. Wagner, yes, he is a doctor, had formed the NATC, which in tum is responsible for coordinating and assigning eligibility of trials clubs to host national rounds. As a result of Dave Russell's recommendation, Wiltz contacted me and indicated that PTR was in consideration for a national. So, after securing a consensus from the PTR membership to pursue this endeavor, in 1973, I traveled to Denver, Colorado, for an NATC meeting. After considering mine and the PTR's performance, the location of our club geographically, what terrain our region offered, as well as other factors, PTR was granted a place on the 1974 National Trials schedule. Time to get to work!

As far as a location, as good as Mackeyville had been for our local events up to this point, it simply would not do for a national. Terrain was fine, but the facility itself just did not feature the space or amenities for an event of a larger scale. Fortunately, I also had another location under consideration. I'd had the idea to host a national for some time and had already been scouting locations. One of them is a place called Roaring Branch Motosport Park, which had been created by Rick and Dot Von Gerbig. Long before today's modern ATV resorts came into existence, Rick and Dot had the idea for just such a facility. They envisioned a riding park, where riders and families could come to camp, ride, and to enjoy the scenic countryside. The Von Gerbigs worked hard to make this a reality and ended up with a really nice place. Easily accessible from the nearby village of Roaring Branch, Pennsylvania, the Von Gerbigs offered everything for a comfortable off-road riding experience, including an on-site restaurant called the Manor House.

An old promotional flyer for the Roaring Branch facility. Note that Rick and Dot were hosting Motocross races on the property, in addition to Trials events.

I had formed a relationship with the Von Gerbigs and really admired what they were working to accomplish. I wanted to help them in their efforts, expand Roaring Branch, and assure its success. No better way to do so than to bring a whole bunch of riders into the place, and the Von Gerbigs really liked the idea of hosting a national trials. And what a great place it is for trials competition. We had four hundred acres to work with, and the terrain featured a 1,000-foot drop from the top of Nail Factory Mountain, with waterfalls cascading down to the valley far below.

Our national took place in September of '74, so the PTR and I had the entire summer to prepare for the event. We laid out some awesome sections, and the loop itself was just amazing. With all the acres to work with, the great elevation change, and a whole series of waterfalls coming down off the mountain, we couldn't go wrong.

Lynne Newmarker Checking
Montessa Mounted Terri McKinney

Checkers are our referees, and are the unsung heroes of Observed Trials. Where would we be without these wonderful folks, who volunteer their time to go out and stand in the woods all day? Not only that, but they hold such great responsibility. Checkers—my hat is off to you. Thank you, one and all!

Things went very well for us at that first national, and as a club, we came away feeling quite encouraged. So encouraged were we in fact that after taking a year off in 1975, PTR hosted another national, held once again on the Von Gerbig's property, in '76. And as the result of a tremendous amount of hard work and effort, that event was just as successful for us as was our first national.

So, there we were, having gone in just a few years from a brand-new club hosting local trials events to having pulled off two very well-regarded nationals. Where to go from there? Why, host a world round, of course! Yes, at that point, I felt as if there was nothing any other club was doing that the PTR couldn't do as well or even better. After all, we had a beautiful facility to work with, which featured some of the absolute best natural trials terrain to be found anywhere, a seasoned, cohesive club, and, of course, we had, me! Ha-ha. Hey, in all modesty, I had it all going on at that point. I knew trials—what it took to provide effectively challenging pro-level sections, I had the local connections to bring all the logistics together, and I had the wherewithal to organize and manage the considerable number of people required to put on an event of the size and scope of an international.

Fédération Internationale Motocycliste

GENÈVE - Suisse

Licence d'officiel international
Licence of international official

№ 2942

Année
Year 19 78

Délivrée par AMERICAN MOTORCYCLIST ASSOCIATION
Granted by

A/to YOUNG Gerry

Adresse

Address

En qualité de Clerk of the Course
As a

The certificate I received from the FIM, confirming me as official Clerk of Course for the event.

I was, of course, working quite closely with the NATC group and successfully lobbied for the PTR to be granted a world round date. We ended up being placed on the 1978 schedule, and so the planning began. Our date was June the 11th of that year, so unlike our first national, there would be no long summer to get everything ready. And we had plenty of challenges during the short time available to us, such as a huge ice storm early in the spring, which bent over every tree on the property, resulting in a terrible mess to clean up. Regardless, the PTR pulled together, and by the first of June, we were ready. And then the rains came.

Our flyer for the '78 World Round. Note my personal address and telephone number. It was all on me.

Yep, early in the week leading up to the event, it began raining. And it rained and it rained. I wasn't panicking at this point but rather just implemented a few additional measures to assure the wet conditions would not cause any undue problems. My brother was contracted to haul in some gravel for the access roads and parking areas in and about the Roaring Branch Park facility, for example, plus we kept a close eye on how the sections were holding up, just to assure no major changes were necessary.

Late in the week, Dick DeBolt, who at the time was the "Sporting Steward" for the NATC, came down from Michigan to assure all was in order and that our sections would be ridable no matter what the weather conditions. With Dick present and observing, I personally rode each section to demonstrate that each was challenging yet manageable. Satisfied, Dick gave the final go-ahead for the course, and we were finally set to go.

Quite fortunately, the weather had actually improved by the time the weekend rolled around and in general conditions were overcast and a bit wet but not really bad at all. Saturday consisted of technical inspection in the parking lot of the Genetti Hotel and later a rider reception in the hotel's dining room. I had done a tremendous amount of planning and preparation to see to it that our event was extra special and well-coordinated. As just one example of this, I insisted that no motorcycles were to be started or operated Sunday morning until after the opening ceremonies were conducted. I wanted ours to be an organized, professional, and dignified event. All total, I had some 250 workers assembled to help manage all facets of the weekend. Besides the sizable PTR presence, by way of donations agreements, I also had on-site members of the local Multiple Sclerosis Society, a big group from a local 4wd club, and even a representation from the area Civil Defense Corps.

Our opening ceremonies at the '78 World Round. There's the Marine Corps Color Guard, and check out that beautiful view in the background. Roaring Branch's mountaintop location made for a terrific venue.

Sunday morning began with foggy conditions, but if anything, the fog actually added to the very special circumstances we had put together. Prior to the start, volunteers pushed all of the competitor's motorcycles into a semicircle. Then the riders paraded in, stood by their machines, and a Marine of Corps Color Guard marched in and played our National Anthem. It was all pretty damn special, and I don't mind admitting that I got pretty choked up as this was all unfolding.

As the event got underway, there was no doubt that we had pulled off yet another great success. The sections were indeed terrifically challenging yet remained totally ridable; spectator access was well-provided for, and our entire support staff worked together to assure that everything went off just as well it possibly could have. There were huge crowds on hand, but we had planned very well to accommodate them. Our parking arrangements worked out well despite the wet conditions, and there were plenty of food vendors and porta cans. The number of spectators who turned out, however, did considerably exceeded our expectations. This became quite evident early on as did the fact that I had completely overlooked the potential need to advise and coordinate with local authorities— as the one and only road leading into the Roaring Branch facility became completely choked with traffic. We did our best to manage the situation and to direct the flow of vehicles coming in, but word evidently got out, and eventually a Sheriff's Department helicopter was dispatched to come out and fly over the event to determine what unexpected event was going on. Whoops! To my best recollection, I believe the attendance figure was right around 3,000, and that's a lot of spectators for an observed trials event!

Lane Leavitt—the next person to win the National Observed Trials Championship, after me. Here, Lane tackles one of the many waterfalls, which were a key part of the '78 World Round. When the riders first went out into the woods to take a look at the sections, they just stared at the waterfalls, possibly wondering how they were ever going to manage such obstacles. All I can say is that—I rode 'em first! Yep, to prove the course was ridable, I had to negotiate every section, to the satisfaction of the NATC's Sporting Steward.

I never expected our world round to be so well-attended, but it was, and what an awesome, successful event we all enjoyed. I could not have been more thrilled and pleased. We concluded the weekend with an awards ceremony back at the Genetti Hotel—a pretty grand place. We hosted a huge sit-down dinner, and I felt at that moment that the entire world had come to Williamsport. The great Bernie Schreiber won the overall, and the little old Pennsylvania Trials Riders club became known worldwide as having hosted an absolute topnotch event. I have never in my life been prouder of any accomplishment.

Another image from the '78 World Round. Bernie Schreiber, on his way to winning the event. Also in this shot are two PTR members—Bill Matheson and Crash Cooper. Sure couldn't have pulled it off without the help of these guys, as well as many other terrific people.

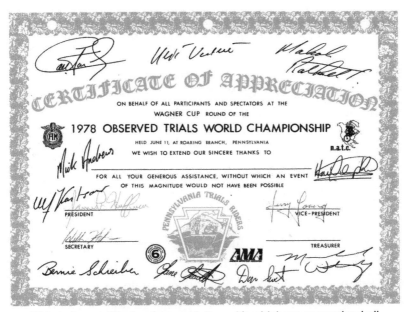

This is the certificate of appreciation with which we recognized all our supporters. There's some pretty famous signatures on there.

Dear Jerry

I am still glowing with pleasure over having ridden your trial. Quite simply, now that I have had some time to reflect on it, it was the best trial I have ever ridden. You are a model and inspiration to us all. Thanks very much.

Wiltz

Among those individuals for whom I reserve my greatest respect is my old friend, Wiltz Wagner. Given Wiltz' level of understanding of the sport of Observed Trials, and his extensive Trials riding experience, it was extremely gratifying to receive this note from him following the '78 World Round.

You've read here where I've used the word "I" a lot in descriptions of how things were put together and organized for all these events—local, national, and international. Of course, PTR members deserve all the credit in the world for truly putting forth a tremendous amount of time and effort in making these events a reality. However, and once again in all modesty, yours truly, Jerry Young, was indeed the driving force behind making it all happen. I wouldn't say such a thing unless it was absolutely true, but I must admit, I really did head up all that you've read about here. Through much of the PTR's formative years, I truly did run things. I was president, secretary, and treasurer. Admittedly, I ran the PTR, period. I'm certainly not trying to sound like a tyrant here, but I knew what was best for the club, and I saw to it that things got done my way, and in the end, the club members had confidence that I knew what I was doing, and it all worked out. For years, I had been driving coast to coast, competing at many events, including multiple world rounds. Having seen how it was "being done," I believed I could put on event not only as good but better than the others. I became certain that my event could be the best.

PTR members must have been generally pleased with my running of the organization as over time we've had upwards of 150 members! We'd maintain twenty or thirty members at any given time, and let me tell you, that's a lot of people to be involved in a local observed trials club out here in mid-state Pennsylvania. And we kept right on conducting events, large and small. The PTR went on to host a total of nine national and two international trials events, each one a considerable success. And for each, I worked hard to assure that ours were special, unique. Why, we had skydivers dropping in at the start of the '87 World Round and all kinds of special activities in conjunction with the trials themselves.

This is a pretty special moment—taken just as I was about the begin the awards presentation at our '87 World Round.

I remained as president of the PTR from its inception until into the 1980s, and I've been back in the fold a time of two even after that, hosting another world round in 1987 and yet another national in 2006. Additionally, I served as an NATC rep for thirty years, traveling to meetings all over the country and passing along my skills and knowledge so that other clubs could hopefully learn from my experiences to improve their own events.

And so, that's how the Pennsylvania Trials Riders club came to be and how we as a group managed to host some of the best trials events in the world. Like I said earlier, plenty of hard work made it all happen. I forged many wonderful relationships during those times and enjoyed experiences I will never forget. It was an exceptionally rewarding time, and I've never felt a moment of regret over the time, money, and effort put forth during all the years I spent with PTR.

CHAPTER 4
Competition

What It Takes to Win

I spent a considerable amount of time thinking about this chapter prior to "putting pen to paper." What does it take to win? Do I know what that "something" may be? Guess I'd never really thought about it before. In fact, it was only when information began to come together in preparation for writing this book that someone pointed out I won my first national championship only a couple of years after having first ridden a motorcycle, ever!

Wow! That really was something. But like I said, I never sat down and actually analyzed myself. Never wondered how the competition-spirit thing works. Since we're talking about it, though, here goes.

As of this moment, I've been riding, and competing (and succeeding, in all modesty), for over fifty years. Wow, again! Fifty years, and I still love riding my motorcycle, still love to compete, and surely still want to win. Good health has a lot to do with it, of course, as I am quite fortunate to still have the physical capabilities to be out there, going for it. And I'm still having fun! Surely, enjoying oneself is key to any activity. If you're not having fun, why bother? Right?

It can be done. However, knowing your bike, having it set up just right, and continually working on your techniques, is what it takes to achieve a level of confidence and skill which permits succeeding against the toughest obstacles.

I think back now to when I was a kid racing around on my bicycle and practicing archery, shooting 250 arrows each night at bottle caps. In those activities, as well as in everything else I've ever done, then and now, I maintain a deep desire to do the very best I can every time. And I do feel satisfaction with my performance—in archery, trials competition, sailing (more on that in another chapter), and numerous other activities. However, I am never fully satisfied. There's always room for improvement. If only I had ridden that one section just a little differently, taken just a little bit different line, gone up that one hill at a slightly different angle, etc.

That number on the front of the bike came as the result
of my resolve to let nothing stand in my way.

Now, I've heard certain individuals say that their driving force is "to annihilate the competition." What apparently motivates them is to do whatever it takes beat everyone and anyone else. Do I feel that way? Yes, I suppose to some extent I do. I mean I want to win, and that means beating the other riders. And yet maybe that outlook is a bit more applicable to "first across the finish line" forms of competition. In observed trials, we are challenged much more by the terrain, as individuals, one rider at a time, through each section. And that's where my attitude of doing the very best I can comes in.

Another example of different attitudes in competition, trials competition, specifically, involves walking sections prior to riding them. I see where some individuals intensely study the other riders' lines and performance, looking for any wrong move or flaw in their competitor's ride.

That works, of course, as you don't want to make the same mistake that caused the rider in front of you to take a five. However, I personally have always studied the sections primarily from the point of view of how I intend to ride them, not particularly based on what the other competitors are doing. Once again, my very best effort. My choice of lines through a section. My study of the obstacles and challenges. And then I go forth and do the very best I can, based on my own decisions, rather than how the other guy or gal rode.

As any Trials rider will tell you, dabs are part of the game. Where and when however, now that's where true skill comes in.

Machine preparation and knowing your bike. So, I've talked about owning the little Triumph Cub for many years and modifying it extensively and how I obviously became very, very familiar with exactly how the bike performs. Observed trials is an exacting sport, so it is essential that your machine of choice functions well and performs exactly as you expect it to. There can't be any surprises in the middle of a section in regard to any aspect of your bike.

Chassis, engine, suspension, brakes, controls, etc., all must be "in tune." How to achieve this? Well, in the case of the Cub, getting it to function ideally in trials competition was a work in progress. As a result, I was always tinkering with it. I knew exactly what was going on with all components of that bike all the time. And aside from some modifications that did not necessarily work out the best, I always knew for certain just what to expect from the bike every time I rode it.

Riding, and training, in adverse conditions, is an absolute must. I am fortunate
in that the area in which I live offers some of the most challenging terrain
a rider might experience, plus plenty of rain and mud, and ice and snow.
Riding in these conditions, rather than shying away from them, contributed
greatly to the level of skill and capabilities which I eventually attainted.

And yet there came the time when I moved on to a new machine.
The Cub went into semiretirement, and I climbed aboard a brand-
new, never-ridden-before, unfamiliar bike. How did I regain the
familiarity I enjoyed with the Cub? Well, two ways, and they're both
pretty obvious. First, I worked on the new bike. Sure, it was new, but
I was not about to take anything for granted. I went through every
component on the bike—top to bottom, front to back, inside and
out. And then I tested the operation of my new acquisition, made
sure everything worked exactly as I wanted it to, how I expected it to,
and how I anticipated it to. And that leads us to the "second thing":
how does one go about testing the performance and operation of a
new bike? Why, riding it, of course. And that leads to practice, practice, practice.

In order to advance to ever higher levels of performance, you must
continually push yourself to overcome the big challenges—the
intimidating obstacles, and then repeat, again and again and again.

In consideration of what I've been talking about here—what it
takes to win, and how I managed to succeed—I believe that as much
as any other factor, it's my constant practicing which has contributed
to many, many successes over the years. And that's not just with the
motorcycles either. Remember, 250 arrows every night!

And so, yes, I ride, a lot. Always have. I'm fortunate to own and
live on a little bit of land, and it is conducive to trials riding, and I
have spent many, many hours right there on my own property riding.
And I have competed, a lot. Bottom line, lots of seat time. And that's
a big part of what it takes. Plus, a bonus to all the riding is achieving
and maintaining a reasonable degree of physical fitness, especially as
it pertains to the rigors specific to observed trials riding. Trials may
not be as physically demanding as motocross or rugby or whatever
the "world's most demanding sports" are, but anyone who has ever
ridden trials competition will attest to just how tough it can be.

Lastly, I must mention "motivation." Certainly, motivation is a primary contributing factor in all that I have accomplished in my life. Without motivation, one simply cannot attain ultimate success or satisfaction with one's performance. And, boy, have I ever been motivated. Looking back over the years, and my achievements, it's hard to express all that I have accomplished without sounding boastful and full of myself. But in truth, I have myself to thank. Getting up and going to work every day, taking care my family, as we all do, but then going on to compete in so many events, all over the country, as well as in the Scottish Six Days, and create the PTR, and put on all those nationals and the international events, and so much, much more. I guess I honestly do have what it takes to win.

I eventually came to receive a bit of notoriety in my hometown. Here's one example of the local paper doing a nice writeup.

The No-Helmet Years

We were invincible!

For those of you unfamiliar with the early days of observed trials riding, yes, it's true: we did not wear helmets while riding or even during competition. Within this book, you will indeed see pictures of me riding with my bare head hanging out in the breeze. Same can be seen in period magazine articles featuring tests of trials bikes and in coverage of trials events.

Yep, that's how it was. Big rocks all over the place and not a helmet to be seen. Couple of notes, here. That's my daughter, Laura Lee, in the striped shirt, at left of picture. Check clenched fists of the little dear—her way of "helping" me through the section. Also, this was at Candytown, in 1972, and was the very day that Jim Ellis showed up with a GRM motorcycle to show me, which eventually led to my association with the GRM brand. Much more on that in another chapter.

Of course, I did wear a helmet in other forms of competition, such as enduros and hare scrambles, as well as when riding on the street. So, why not while participating in observed trials? I'm not sure what the general outlook was, but for me, and my contemporaries, we just did not consider trials to be particularly dangerous. You know, low speeds and all that. Can you imagine? With the constant risk of bashing one's head on a rock, hitting a tree, looping out, and getting landed on by your own motorcycle, or any one of innumerable other potential hazards, we did not feel helmets to be "necessary." It's all quite laughable now when looking back on the dangers we exposed ourselves to.

One thing's for sure—you could certainly see our facial expressions. Not to mention hair flyin' in the breeze.

There was in fact an entire culture which existed at the time, involving trials riders sporting all sorts of different caps and hats in place of helmets. Yep, we'd see stroker caps, fishing hats, Navy caps, and all manner of soft, floppy sun hats perched on rider's heads. I typically wore no head covering at all although in honor of my produced-in-Mexico GRM trials bike, I actually competed in some events while wearing a big, ol' sombrero.

And there's the sombrero. Helped me to stand out, that's for sure. Note the pretty tough section, and yet I am not even covering the clutch. We didn't know to use the clutch at this point! Wasn't until Mick Andrews came over and demonstrated his techniques that we rode any way other than by just using momentum to get through sections.

Now, aside from the perceived absence-of-danger outlook, another reason for going without helmets was the general feeling that observed trials required the rider to be unencumbered by restrictions imposed by a helmet. It was considered that, burdened by a helmet, the rider's vision, hearing, and "sense of his (or her) surroundings" would be inhibited. Right or wrong, no one wanted to give up any advantage to the competition. And, of course, I felt the same way. I wanted to be able to "hear" how close I came to some tree in a tight section, for example, just before rubbing right up against said tree and scraping half the skin off my ear. Ouch! But such was the price of success in observed trials, or so we felt.

Eventually, of course, the sanctioning bodies began requiring helmets to be worn in competition. Yes, but what kind of helmet to utilize? Certainly, we knew what was needed—something light-weight, ventilated, non-vision restrictive, and with an abbreviated (if any) visor. It took a while for specialty trials helmets to become available, so in the interim, it was left up to the individual rider to come up with something effective and accepted. Some guys simply went back to the old half-helmets, often with a canvas lower section. I even once saw a rider wearing a helmet intended for use in equestrian riding and competition. Either way, those types of helmets featured nothing in way of provisions for ventilation. And in the low-speed, stop-and-go, strenuous world of trials riding, they were bloody, bloody hot.

My first helmet was one intended for street riding. It was obtrusive, heavy, non-vented, and about to cook my brains out while riding off-road. I remedied some of the bulk by literally cutting the front of the helmet, plus improved ventilation by drilling a bunch of big, ol' holes in the top of the thing. The end result worked quite well, but I eventually began getting the hairy eyeball from competition officials and so decided to seek out and invest in an honest-to goodness motorcycle helmet, one geared to the demands of observed trials riding.

Ok, so here I am, finally with a helmet on—my modified job. Worked out quite well, actually. Note advancement to much more comprehensive riding gear at this point, thanks to my friends, Frank Esposito and Bob Fahnestock, of Ossa East, out of Downington, Pennsylvania, who were my sponsors at the time.

And the rest is history. Needless to say, these days, the sport of observed trials is blessed with all manner of effective, superlight headgear designed specifically for our purposes. We're very fortunate to have access to modern helmets as well as all the other safety gear on the market today. One look at those old pictures of me competing in what amounted to street clothes is clear testament to how far we've come.

CHAPTER 6

The '72 Championship Season

I didn't know I'd won!

A big part of the reason I began competing in, and eventually pro-moting, observed trials events is quite simply because there were (and are) a lot of trials events held in the part of the country where I live. Indeed, Eastern Pennsylvania's AMA District 6 represents a hotbed of trials competition and as a result draws a lot of competitors, and not only from within the district, but also from neighboring, eastern seaboard states. Suffice to say, there was, and, of course, still are, a lot of very skilled riders vying for points in District 6 events.

Now, a couple of things to get straight right up front. First, much of the content of this book is drawn from my own personal memory of events which took place some fifty years ago! Additionally, attempts to verify my recollection of times, dates, places, and exacting details have been made difficult by inconsistencies in documentation dating to the period. Remember, there was no official AMA Observed Trials National Championship before they awarded the title to me. Mine was indeed the first. However, current online references do not nec-essarily reflect or include (all) the facts. Specifically, and with all due respect to the individuals responsible, as of the writing of this book, the AMA's own online documentation lists Lane Levitt as having won the first AMA National Observed Trials Champion in 1974!

What happened in 1973? And, interestingly, Jerry Young was recognized by the AMA as the 1972 National Observed Trials Champion even though I won the title as the result of points gathered in 1971! Confusing? You bet. At the time this book went to print, we were still working to address these inconsistencies, but so far, no luck. One thing's for sure, folks, I won that title and have the plaques from the AMA to prove it. Enough said!

So, let's back up a bit to the 1970 season. I was really into observed trials competition by this time. Had the old Cub working pretty darn well, and even though I'd turned thirty, I was in good shape, was riding better than ever, and my confidence was at an all-time high. I was riding just about every trials event I could manage to get myself to and had gotten to the point where I was in the hunt for the overall win just about every weekend. I wasn't chasing points though. Nope, I was just going out and riding every single section, in every event, to the absolute best of my ability, going for the win at each of those individual events.

Regardless of my own, personal ignorance of district points accumulation, at some point, I became aware of, or was informed by someone, that I was leading in the tally for that year's District 6 championship. And with good luck, good riding, consistency, and determination, I carried that advantage through to the end of the season. So, off we go to the District 6 awards banquet, and, man, I'm pumped up! I mean, this was a big deal. District 6 was supported by a lot of promoters, events, and competitors, and their banquet was right on par (to my understanding) with the AMA's national awards soiree. Observed trials certainly was modestly represented by comparison to the road-riding groups, flat-track and road-racing contingents, and so forth, but still it was going to be a big deal for me to get called up there for the number one district award in my category. Ah, but guess what? All the awards get handed out, but no mention of Jerry Young. I was mystified. Finally got in touch with "the powers that be." Records were checked and numbers were counted, and sure enough, I had earned more points than anyone else in District 6 observed trials competition. "So, why no award?" I asked. "Well, apparently you never paid the ten bucks and registered for the district championship" was the reply.

I was stunned. And angry. Angry at myself for having over-looked such a minor detail as the need for an additional registration at some point in the season, plus angry because no one at any point came forward and brought this to my attention. However, I soon gathered myself up and turned the anger into determination. Oh, yes, I was going to *win* the next year's championship. There was no doubt in my mind.

On to the 1971 season, right? Well, sort of. Interestingly, the '71 season actually kicked off in November of 1970 and wrapped up the following October. So, November in the Pennsylvania woods, and you can just imagine what it was like. Yep, cold, wet, mud, snow, and ice-covered rocks. Didn't bother me one bit though. I'm an out-doorsy kind of guy anyway and used to Pennsylvania's weather no matter what the time of year. And my Cub thrived on the challeng-ing conditions. Small, lightweight, and with that marvelously flexible little four-stroke engine, I could chug it down to virtually zero revs, and the thing would just keep pulling.

Remember, this was the old days, and before outsiders, such as Mick Andrews, came over from across the pond and demonstrated some alternative techniques, we didn't even utilize the clutch to aid us. Nope, it was, as I have previously described, all about throttle control and balance.

By this time, I'd put out of my mind the frustration of getting skunked out of the 1970 District 6 championship. In fact, I was not even thinking about points. Instead, I was just having fun! Yep, I was going out to every meet and riding my motorcycle and enjoying the heck out of myself; I also happened to be winning a lot. And make no doubt, the competition was fierce. As I recall, the toughest guys to beat that year included fellow District 6 riders, such as Pete Slesser, who rode a heavily-modified, white-tanked Yamaha DT1; Duke Leedy, on a Montesa Cota; and Lester Bergen, who campaigned a Bultaco. Another really good rider was Brian Jones, who came in from New Jersey. Brian rode, if memory serves, a Hodaka. These names represent just a few of the really skilled guys who poured in from all over to compete in District 6. Plenty of them were mounted on bikes which were designed specifically for observed trials too. And there I was, on my funky little Cub, which I'll tell you, was pretty cobby. Yeah, it was built strictly for functionality. Cosmetics were not even a consideration. Note that my Cub was not a loner, however. There was this guy named James Foster, who rode for Triumph, and had an actual prepped-by-the-factory Cub. And boy, James's Cub was all slick and pretty, and James himself wore really fancy gear, and he did all right.

But week after week, meet after meet, Jerry Young was the guy to beat, on that grubby, chuffing, and smoking little Cub. People would come over while we were sitting around in the pits and just be all over the Cub, trying to figure out how exactly it seemed to work so well. Now, here's where I need to put modesty aside a bit. The Cub was good. It performed well, and it was reliable. And I worked on it all the time. Not that it needed a lot of maintenance or repair as observed trials, especially in those days, was not at all hard on equipment. Instead, I was constantly tweaking the bike, continually tinkering to assure it was providing every advantage over, or at least keeping me on par with, the competition. And about that tinkering, some of it was minor, such as a gearing change or fiddling with the carb. But other times I would go so far as to make alterations to the frame! Yep, right in the middle of the season, I would periodically get it in my head that the steering head angle needed to be adjusted, or that the motor needed to be moved forward or rearward, to affect balance or steering. And the torches would come out, and the frame would be cut and welded and then back together in time for the next event. But with that said, and given that my Cub did indeed function quite well, the primary key to my success was me! I rode, and practiced, everyday literally.

Soon as I got home from work, I was on the bike, out in the woods, riding sections, right up until it got too dark to see. And then I would get out in the open and ride some more until I couldn't see at all. And this was in all conditions too. I didn't ride just when it was nice outside. Nope, cold, rain, you name it, I was out there riding. Now, I am fortunate in that I've got some trials-conducive terrain right on my own property. Right out the back door, I had five sections laid out, tough stuff, too, and I worked at cleaning all five sections, five times every night. Practice makes perfect, as they say, and friends, I got good!

And we progressed through the season. Nothing particularly spectacular comes to mind as, of course, in trials; there is no bar-to-bar action, no stupendous hole shots, or huge crashes. Instead, it was a matter of getting out to every event and riding every single section, on every loop, skillfully, and, as I've said before, to the absolute very best of my ability.

I kept to myself mostly, focused for the most part on what I wanted to accomplish. If there was any one person I hung out with on a regular basis, that would have been Pete Slesser. I wasn't being aloof or snobbish or anything, just quiet and laid back, enjoying myself all the while too! Actually, it was kind of fun being reserved and just let everyone wonder about how this poor boy with the old, crude, hand-built motorcycle could beat them week after week.

I never thought of being anything special either. Instead, my outlook was that I was having fun, the Cub was working well, and through all that consistent practicing, I simply happened to be able to, at that particular time, outperform the other competitors. Little did I realize that my presence, and riding, actually did have a considerable influence on other people. In fact, it was not until years later, at a banquet, that Bob Howard, one of my old chums from back then, stepped up and spoke about how he evidently picked me out as the rider to emulate back when he was still up and coming in the sport of trials. Bob described in his little presentation that he had studied all the top riders at various events back then and eventually settled on me, Jerry Young, as the rider he could learn from the most. Bob explained that his impression of me was that of a "studied and calculating competitor, very exacting in how I checked out sections and then rode them." It was most unexpected and extremely flattering. I had no idea that my efforts impacted anyone! And for what it's worth, Bob went on to become a very skilled observed trials rider and, among many other accomplishments, rode the Scottish Six Days Trial no less than nine times.

Well, the '71 season wound down to its conclusion at the end of October. I'd not had a problem all year. I had stayed healthy, turned out for all the events I could, and that old Cub just keep runnin' as reliable as could be. Note that there were a lot of events too. Without digging through all the back issues of *Cycle News*, I do believe that we rode upward of forty-five rounds that year. Amazingly, I actually still found time to ride events outside of observed trials, most notably the Berkshire Two-Day Trials, and that's a story in itself.

Off to the District 6 banquet then, and this time by gosh, I'd made absolute damn sure I had paid the lousy ten bucks and registered for my points to be calculated. Ha-ha. And I'll mention once again just what a large and well-attended event the District 6 banquet was and, of course, still is. Just a big, ol' bunch of people in attendance, and everyone's all dressed up, especially the district officials. They all had on matching red blazers, and everything was just all official and as impressive as could be. Now, you'd think that after all I had been through, all the time and effort, all the traveling, and events, and riding, and practicing, and the frustration of missing out on the 1970 championship that the actual receipt of my award that night would have been my great and shining moment. The absolute pinnacle of all that I had worked for. Well, of course, it was, to an extent. However, the actual awards process was really just a formality. Sure, I was very, very pleased with myself, and extremely happy that I'd accomplished all that I had set out to do. And yet there we were the trials guys just one small group, at one table, over in the corner of this huge room full of people. And all of us really just wanted to get through the awards presentation and get on with the partying and dancing. So, after sitting there through many, many other winners being called up to receive their awards, all the other competitors, and I don't know how many awards for road riders, my name was finally called; I received my recognition, and that was it. Off we went to drink and party and have a good time, and Jerry Young was the 1971 District 6 Observed Trials Champion. Hot dog!

There we are at the District 6 banquet, with our hardware. That's
Pete Slesser on my left, who finished in second place.

So, what about the national championship? Well, talk about
anticlimactic; remember that there was at that time no AMA national
award for observed trials. Such a designation, or title, simply was not
on anyone's mind. There was no national championship series, of
course. It was instead, riders in districts all over the country competing for individual victories at any given event, and if they had
signed up, their points were being tabulated toward individual district awards. However, unbeknownst to us, the AMA had that year
elected to gather up the points awarded to each rider, in each district,
from all of observed trials competition nationwide. And once all the
adding up had taken place, one Jerry Young, out in District 6, had
the highest number of accumulated points, and so let's designate him
as "national champion." Wowee!

I didn't have a clue. No one contacted me. I did not receive
any notification or an invitation to the AMA National awards banquet. One day, this packet simply arrived in the mail and inside were

two "number-one" plaques—one to represent the Eastern Regional Championship and the other for the national title. I never made a big deal out of it, and there was not much recognition or acknowledgment from my peers.

I never looked into determining why my '72 National title was designated "Amateur" rather than "Professional". Possibly it was because our events did not pay anything to the riders. I do know that Wiltz Wagner, always the visionary, preferred the amateur status, as he had hopes that Observed Trials would at some point be included in the Olympics.

So, there you have it, folks, 1972 AMA National Observed Trials Champion. In the end, did I travel the country, competing in a complete series of national events, pitting myself against the best riders from throughout the country? No, I did not. However, I did ride some forty-five events in one year, in all conditions, on an old, hand-built trail bike converted into a trials bike, with absolutely zero outside support, against some of the best, most dedicated trials riders anywhere, many of whom were years younger than me, all while holding down a job and raising a family. I earned those points, and I won that title. Of that I am damned sure.

CHAPTER 7
The GRM Experience

My time as a factory-supported rider.

Much attention has been paid recently, and rightfully so, to motorcycling pioneers. such as John Penton, Edison Dye, Preston Petty, and others. However, there's another name, which you're unlikely to be familiar with although this individual also played a considerable part in development of our sport as we know it today.

The man to whom I refer is Bill Grapevine. Born in Kansas in 1931, Bill lived through the Great Depression, served in the US Navy, worked as a jet aircraft mechanic, and road raced motorcycles, plus competed in desert racing, motocross, and observed trials. As early as 1963, Bill was building and selling his own purpose-built observed trials bikes. Beginning in 1965, he organized a Motorcycle Industry Council-sanctioned "National Trials Championship," which ran for three years. Bill also organized and put on one of the first international motocross events in the United States, which took place in 1967, at Bill's own facility—Aztec Park, near Sedan, Kansas.

Through the late 1960s, Bill continued his efforts to design, produce, and sell his own brand of motorcycles, which he called Mavericks—usually powered by Hodaka engines. Later, he built and campaigned a 125 motocrosser, powered by a Carabella engine and enjoyed considerable success with the bike in 1968 and 1969. Encouraged by this success, Bill established Grapevine Racing Motors in 1970. Together with his machinist friend, Charlie Hill, Bill spent a year at the Carabella facility in Mexico City, working on engineering and design of 125cc and 200cc race bikes, which Carabella had agreed to produce. Once satisfied that their product was ready, Bill and Charlie returned to the US with two prototypes, hoping to interest dealers in California and secure some orders for the bikes.

Unfortunately, the deal with Carabella fell through, and Bill decided to go a different route. He next met with Mexican manufacturer, Moto Islo, with a proposal for them to build observed trials bikes of Bill's design, utilizing existing Moto Islo motors, punched out to 215cc, per Bill's request. A deal was struck, and in time, GRM trials bikes went into production.

I first became aware of GRM motorcycles in 1972. I had retired my venerable old Triumph Cub at the end of the '71 season and was campaigning a brand-new Ossa MAR (Mick Andrews Replica). I was sportin' the National Number One plate out front of the Plonker, the bike was working out great, and I was loving life. Then a fellow named Jim Ellis showed up at Candytown one weekend with this GRM in the back of his truck and asked me to check it out. We unloaded it out of Jim's truck, and the first thing I thought was, *Uh-oh, this thing feels heavy.* But the bike looked good. It sported a headlight and taillight, was named the "Trialsmaster," and was quite purposeful-looking. Jim offered for me to take a ride on the bike, so I fired it up and rode around a bit. Jim watched as I managed a couple of obstacles with no problem then easily climbed the GRM up onto a big rock. When I returned the bike, Jim asked what I thought. I told him that I thought it could work, and Jim loaded up and away he went.

DESIGNED BY BILL GRAPEVINE AND MANUFACTURED BY MOTO ISLO S.A. OF SATILLO, MEXICO

⸎⸎⸎⸎

THE ONLY 250cc CLASS TRIALS BIKE THAT USES A FRAME MADE OF AIRCRAFT QUALITY 4130 STEEL TUBING IMPORTED INTO MEXICO FROM THE U.S.A.

Grapevine Racing Motors, Inc.

750 E. PAWNEE
WICHITA, KANSAS 67211

ISLO
TRIALSMASTER

Weight overall	219 pounds
Frame type	single front down tube
Front tire size	275x21
Rear tire size	400x18

SUSPENSION:

Front fork	Ceriani or Betor
Rear shocks	Boge

FOR INFORMATION CALL
316—263-7285

ENGINE:

Engine Type	Two stroke, piston port, single cylinder.
Horsepower @ rpm	18 @ 5900
Torque @ rpm	17.2 ft/lb @ 4800
Bore and stroke	65mm x 65mm
Displacement	215cc
Compression ratio	9.1:1
Carburetion	26mm Mikuni
Ignition	Flywheel magneto

TRANSMISSION:

Number of speeds	four
Primary drive	Single row chain
Clutch type	Wet, multi-disc
Final drive	Chain, 5/8x5/16

CHASSIS:

Length, overall	80 inches
Wheelbase	52 inches
Ground clearance	10.5 inches

The official GRM spec sheet typed up by Bill Grapevine himself. That's Bill's own telephone number listed at the bottom. Check out how he specified that the tubing for the frame was "imported into Mexico from the U.S.A."!

I didn't give the situation much more thought until Jim called me about a week later. He explained that he was an investor in GRM, and they needed a top rider to compete aboard and promote the new bike. Jim told me that he had spoken to Bill Grapevine and con-

69

vinced him that I was the man they wanted on the bike. I was advised to expect a call from Bill to work out the details.

Now, I didn't know it at the time, but it turns out that Jim Ellis was much more than simply an investor in the entire GRM endeavor. I later found that Jim's involvement dates back to 1964 when he graduated from college in Maine, with a commission in the United States Air Force. A month after receiving his diploma, Jim climbed into his 1930 Ford Sport Coupe and traveled to Sheppard Air Force Base in Wichita Falls, Texas, to report as a brand-new trainee. Following initial training there, Jim was then assigned to McConnell Air Force base, located in Wichita, Kansas. Jim's assignment there was working "underground" in the military's Titan 2 missile silos! With a twenty-four-hour on, forty-eight-hour off schedule, Jim had a lot of free time on his hands, and having purchased a '58 Triumph Tiger Cub, he began hanging around the local motorcycle shops. It was during this time, along about 1965 or 1966, that Jim made the acquaintance of Bill Grapevine.

As a young, ambitious fellow at that time, Jim became quite interested in Bill's exploits. After all, here was a man who was working on building and marketing his own motorcycles as well as seeking to host international-level motorcycle racing events right there in Kansas. And so, it was that Jim eventually involved himself with Bill's various ambitions.

It was in November of 1967 then that Bill Grapevine hosted his FIM-sanctioned International Motocross event, which Jim helped with considerably. This event was an early stop on the very first tour by the CZ and Husqvarna factory teams as they sought to introduce Americans to world-class Motocross. Their noteworthy riders included former world champion Torsten Hallman of Sweden, then-current world champion Joel Robert of Belgium, future world champion Roger Decoster of Belgium, British national champion Dave Bickers, plus Ake Jonsson and Steffan Eneqvist, both from Sweden. Bill also hosted observed trials events at his Kansas facility, in which Jim first competed in trials aboard a Bultaco Matador. This is also about the time that Bill began to get quite serious about mass-producing his own motorcycles. Plans were drawn up, and Bill began creating a prototype frame. As Jim tells it, Bill Grapevine never did have much money. He did take conventional jobs periodically but only worked enough "to feed himself," spending the rest of his time pursuing his various projects and dreams. This is where Jim stepped up and gave Bill $8,000 as an investment into the fledgling GRM company. That would be about $50,000 today. Not a small amount of money!

After the Carabeila deal fell through, it took until 1972 before Bill, working next with the Mexican Moto Iso company, actually got the first GRMs into production. Jim Ellis's investment was long gone, but Bill had talked a Wichita bank into writing him a business loan, providing enough money for the first production run of fifty motorcycles. And the bikes were produced and were shipped to a warehouse in Wichita, where Bill had arranged for them to be stored. But that's when the enterprise ran into a snag. They had gotten this far—designed, engineered, and arranged production of fifty motorcycles, yet they had no customers. Neither Jim nor Bill, or Bill's partner, Charlie Hill, had worked at marketing the bikes. They had no dealers set up, no one in line to purchase the bikes, and few prospects. It was time to get after that end of the business!

Somehow, Bill got *Cycle World* magazine to test a GRM. Observed trials was being considered at that time as possibly the "next big thing," so there was a general interest within the motorcycling public, and the motorcycle publications, to give these new bikes a try. Unfortunately, *Cycle World's* review of the bike was quite negative. The GRM's 215cc, two stroke engine, which we believe was an Italian design that Moto Islo had secured, was indeed very sturdy. Its design features included a double-wall crankcase and four main bearings. But it was also very heavy, due in part to a cast iron cylinder. Plus, it had only four speeds, and the internal ratios were quite tall—not at all conducive for observed trials. Bill addressed the gear ratio issue the only way he could, by fitting a huge rear sprocket. Additionally, *Cycle World* found fault with the GRM's fiberglass. Not so much the tank but the rear fender, and especially the skid plate, were considered much too fragile for trials work. And there were the brakes, or the lack thereof. We never quite figured out why, but the GRM's brake lining material was slightly slippery.

Interestingly, the front hub is an exact copy of a Honda unit, so while the brakes had basic capability, they just didn't work. Plus, the rear brake lever was tucked in such that it was nearly impossible to find while riding. And there were other component issues, such as the kick-start lever. It was made of iron and tended to break. And *Cycle World* definitely pointed out the GRM's weight. If I remember correctly, the first GRM I had come in at about 225 lbs. ready to ride, and that's a lot for a trials bike, even one produced in the GRM's era. My modern Sherco weighs only 155 lbs., and even my Tiger Cub, a converted road-legal, four-stroke, trail bike, weighs just 205. In addition to that heavy engine and components, such the iron kick-starter, the bike's frame was very heavy as well. Bill Grapevine had spec'd the GRM frame to be constructed of 4130 chrome moly steel, but by the time it reached production, somehow the frame material ended up made from what we called "water pipe." One of the few aspects of the GRM with which *Cycle World* found favor were the forks. They were Cerianis, or at least copies of Cerianis, and actually worked quite well.

Regardless of the panning *Cycle World* gave the bike, pursuit of prospective dealers got underway in earnest. One dealer which Jim Ellis signed up was a fellow named Marty Guide, a District 6 rider, who lived near Scranton, Pennsylvania. Marty came up with several improvements for his GRMs, which he never shared with Jim Ellis or Bill Grapevine. Marty discarded the factory fiberglass skid plate and made up a replacement out of aluminum diamond plate. Marty also addressed another problem, which we knew about right from the start—the GRMs did not possess sufficient ground clearance for trials work. Marty improved upon this shortcoming by cutting away the lower part of the frame's downtube and raised the front of the engine. Since GRMs used the engine as a stressed member, this was a fairly simple process. Jim Ellis tells me that Marty didn't actually own a shop. Instead, he worked out of one crowded corner of his real business—a mill, where Marty pulverized jaw breakers candy for their sugar content, which in turn was sold as an ingredient for cattle feed. Marty's enthusiastic riding techniques were his primary sales tools, and Jim recalls that Marty ended up selling about nine GRMs, which we believe were just used for trail riding as we never saw any of Marty's bikes at trials events.

While Marty was doing his thing out on the East Coast to improve GRM performance in order to (hopefully) sell some of them, Jim Ellis was likewise attempting to address known issues with the bikes. Case in point, those iron kick-starters. Jim found by chance that the kick-start lever from an Ossa Stiletto not only matched the GRM's spline size but would also travel through its arc without banging into anything. Jim then reached out to John Taylor, then importer of Ossa motorcycles in the US, and cut a deal to purchase 100 Stiletto kick-starters at $10.00 each. This was all right out of Jim's pocket. Bill Grapevine then worked to swap out the kickers on GRM's before they left the distribution warehouse, or at least a hundred of them anyway. Marty Guide had also discovered that Triumph Tiger Cub brake linings would fit onto the GRM brake shoes. This modification improved braking, but GRMs still had lousy stopping power. Mine sure did. Jim's next step was to fit his own bike with a compression release. Utilization of a compression release to aid or supplement braking was not at all uncommon back then, so we readily adapted the technique in trials competition.

Another potential GRM supporter, Carl Peters, from upstate New York, was given a GRM to ride. Carl modified his bike by installing a flywheel weight, which he had machined out of brass, and managed to produce in a size which would fit inside the existing GRM's engine cover. This mod was quite beneficial, but Carl just never quite got on board and ended up returning his bike after just a few months. After taking possession of the bikes, Jim Ellis inspected Carl's handiwork on the flywheel weights and found that Carl had, as a bit of a joke, stamped into it "MMS&A," which we later found out stood for "Moreland (Carl's hometown) Manure Spreader and Aerospace." Quite the funny guy, that Carl.

So, back to my initial introduction to Jim Ellis and the GRM motorcycle and Jim's indication that they wanted me to ride the bike and represent GRM. I was pretty darned excited about the whole thing. Heck, here I was just a poor working fellow, who until recently had been competing entirely on my own dime, on a hand-modified trail bike, and now all of a sudden, a motorcycle manufacturer wants me to ride for them! And Bill called the next week, and we did indeed work out a deal. Now, I wasn't going to be a paid rider or anything like that, but Bill said they were going to provide me with a free, brand-new motorcycle, and that was good enough for a start!

Here's a pretty nice image of the bike as it was delivered from the factory. Note the full lighting kit.

I took possession of the GRM, sold my Ossa, and began competing on the new bike. And I achieved respectable success with it. We did certainly begin modifying the GRM right off the bat as described earlier in the chapter. To start with, we raised the front of the engine to increase ground clearance, installed one of Carl Peters' flywheel weights, tossed that fiberglass skid plate, bolted up one of Marty Guide's diamond plate ones, and swapped out the stock carb for a modified Mikuni. Once tuned effectively, the Mikuni, along with the flywheel weight, enabled my GRM to lug down to almost zero revs without stumbling or stalling. And remember, low-rev performance was absolutely critical at this point because, as I've mentioned a couple of times now, we had yet to figure out how to effectively utilize the clutch at super slow speeds. Plus, I installed and utilized a compression release to supplement the GRM's lousy brakes. As for the GRM's weight, I couldn't do anything about that thick-walled, heavy frame, but I did go after the cast iron cylinder. Drilled that thing all full of holes. I actually shaved some five pounds from the bike's overall weight, just from lightning up the jug. I also drilled holes in the GRM's outer case although in hindsight that wasn't such a great idea as the holes allowed the thing to pack full of mud. After all this work was performed, I had the bike working pretty well. Keep in mind, however, and in all modesty, it was my personal skills which helped to offset the GRM's shortcomings. I was after all the reigning national champion and was truly at the top of my game.

Grapevine Racing Motors is serious about trials.
... so is National '1'

• Superior Balance and Handling	• Mikuni Carburetor
• 4130 Frame and Swingarm	• Ceriani Forks
• Adjustable Turning Radius Stops	• Boge Shocks
• FWD Speedometer & Odometer	• Primary Kick Start
• U.S.F.S. Approved Spark Arrestor	• Lights & Kill Button

For complete specs, photos, prices contact

GRAPEVINE RACING MOTORS, INC.
750 East Pawnee
Wichita, Kansas 67211   (316) 263-7285

Dealer and Rep Inquiries Invited

*Jerry Young, Current AMA NATIONAL #1 TRIALS RIDER on his GRM

Well, would you look at that—there I am, featured in a national advertising promotion, for a motorcycle manufacturer. These "promo" series of photos were taken, not in competition, but in an area just down the street from my house.

Check that riding gear. Button-down shirt, sheepskin vest, jeans,
no helmet, no gloves. At least I had my Full Bores on.

Jim Ellis, meanwhile, was very anxious to promote GRMs and in turn sell some of them. My performance in local trials was encouraging, and the new bike was getting attention, but Jim figured that we needed to compete in some events beyond District 6 to get more exposure for the bike. On Father's Day of 1973, Jim arranged for us to travel to Michigan to compete in a two-day trial hosted by the Michigan Ontario Trials Association, which was being promoted as a "national championship" event. Considering the gap between the AMA Championship I was awarded as the result of points accumulated in the 1971 season and the next official AMA National Championship, which was not awarded until 1974, it would stand to reason that these MOTA events, held in '72 and '73, represented "the championship" during those two years.

In the fall of '73 then, I was given a real treat, when Jim Ellis and I flew out to Colorado, where I competed in the Ute Cup—my first time at that event. Bill Grapevine was there, waiting for us. He had brought three GRMs, each set up slightly differently from the others, and I was given my choice of which one to ride. Boy, this factory-supported-rider thing was great! Overall, riding the Ute Cup was an amazing experience. Having never been west of the

Mississippi, and certainly having never ridden in the kind of terrain the Rocky Mountains featured, I was very excited about it all. And to top it all, who did I find myself next to as we prepared to get underway but the one and only Sammy Miller! And Sammy was giving the GRM a very thorough looking-over. I waited to hear what questions or comments Miller might ask about the bike, but in the end, all he said was, "At least it's got good forks." And with that we headed out onto the first loop.

Still in jeans at this point, but I finally have a helmet on, in this case specifically due to the event. I'm competing here in the Ute Cup—my first time. The Rocky Mountain Trials Association required helmets, due in no small part to the many high-speed trails in between sections. The Ute Cup events are incredible—12,000 foot altitude, and incredible terrain. More modifications to the bike are evident here—a Mikuni carb, plus I've changed out the stock fiberglass front fender for a plastic one, and installed a smaller rear sprocket.

I did enjoy riding the Ute Cup very much due in no small part to the fact that none of it was on my dime. Regardless, it was quite a learning experience and whetted my appetite for competing in more trials events outside of my native Pennsylvania and surrounding areas. It was also great challenging myself against high-ranking competitors, such as Sammy Miller with whom I rubbed elbows all that weekend. Sammy's skills, techniques, and methods were really interesting. In one section, for example, I took note of a special little trick Sammy employed, one which could make the difference between winning and losing. All the Ute Cup's sections were outlined with little flags sticking up out of the ground on thin metal rods, the kind you see used to mark where buried cable or pipe is going to be laid. With many riders competing in the event, the favored lines eventually became pretty torn up, muddy, and rutted.

After we walked this one section, Sammy took his turn to ride it. I was still walking and finding my own line and so took note of Miller's progress. At one turn, most all the previous riders had gone right up to the edge of the flag-topped pins, and, of course, there was a muddy rut there as a result. In order to provide himself the advantage of a fresh, clean line, Miller had stepped on one of the pins, bending the flag over, and providing himself with just a single tire-width of fresh surface. Very cleverly, Sammy had pushed the boundaries of the section to his advantage. Did he break the rules? Not for me to say. Either way, it was an interesting play on our game of two-wheeled precision.

So went my first years' experience as a factory-supported rider, and I've gotta tell you, it was great! A nice, new, although somewhat flawed bike paid trips to ride in places I'd never even visited, and all the while with the number one plate on the front of my bike. Although I hoped the situation would continue for some time, the writing was on the wall, as they say. Despite sincere efforts to get other riders interested in the GRM, I personally had sold all of just two bikes. I wasn't sure how well Jim and Bill were doing, but it couldn't have been much better than me. Sure enough, by 1974, the bank in Wichita figured out that Bill wasn't selling many bikes and shut down the whole affair. They took possession of all remaining inventory, and Grapevine Racing Motors was effectively out of business. I thought that was the end of it, but as it turns out, there was to be a second go-round of the GRM saga.

Out on a loop, between sections. Check out that neat GRM jersey.
If you look closely in this picture, you can see that the bike's front
hub was sourced from Honda—or at least was a Honda copy.

Evidently, there was a fellow from Pennsylvania who approached the Wichita bank which had financed Bill Grapevine's manufacturing endeavors. And this person evidently, somehow, someway, convinced the bank to release Bill's entire inventory to him. Jim Ellis and I have both given this considerable thought, but neither of us have been able to recall this guy's name. Neither do we have anything written down in regard to the situation. So, the new owner of all the GRM inventory shall remain unnamed here, and may be that's for the better because to the best of our understanding, the Wichita bank never received a dime of payment from this fellow. Whatever the case, I found out where the bikes were and went over to visit the guy. Wasn't sure what I was looking to accomplish, but I at least wanted to find out what the deal was. Well, wouldn't you know that after some discussion about what effort I had played the previous year in marketing the bikes, Mr. No Name and I struck a deal to continue the effort! I came away with yet another new bike and $2,500 in cash to support further promotional efforts! How do you like that?

My "new" GRM was an updated version of the first one I'd ridden as Bill had implemented changes and updates to the bikes during the various production runs which took place throughout 1973. This bike stood out cosmetically from the first model as the result of fancy gold lettering, making up the GRM logo on the tank plus some gold trim on the rear fender. And there were mechanical upgrades as well, such as a longer swingarm and a different rear engine mount arrangement. We decided to go for broke this time around in the marketing, and, what with some funding behind me, I planned two big trips in 1974.

Here's an advertisement for the very first U.S. round of an International Observed Trials event. Reprinted with permission of Cycle World magazine.

First off, we'd known for some time that the first-ever US round of an FIM-sanction International Observed Trials event was to take place in January of '74, all the way out in southern California, sponsored by *Cycle*

World magazine, and held at world famous Saddleback Park. Together with Dave Russel and Bill Matheson, we drove all the way out there in Dave's van, with our bikes in the back. One interesting note was that this took place during the 1973–1974 "gas crisis," during which time the availability of fuel was uncertain. Fortunately for us, Dave's van was equipped with two auxiliary fuel tanks, providing some assurance that we had plenty of range in case we'd have to do some searching to find a gas station that was both open and had gas available.

Well, we made it all the way cross-country and arrived on schedule out at Saddleback Park—my first time there. As far as the event goes, any student of observed trials competition in the United States will be familiar with the fact that the event was an absolute mess. Although the promoters certainly put forth their very best effort to make the best of the terrain available, they simply could not be prepared for Mother Nature intervening so strongly. In short, it rained. Quite unusually for the area, a considerable amount of rain fell, both before and during the event. And all that water turned the course into a real mess. Everyone struggled, including me, of course. There were big bottlenecks at many of the tougher sections, and many riders finished outside their allotted time. Alan Lampkin won that day, in part because he risked taking a five at one or more backed up sections and managed to finish on time.

I wish I could remember more about that event because it certainly was historic, being the first-ever US world round. Unfortunately, as bad as the conditions were, and the fact that Saddleback's terrain did not lend itself very well to trials sections, the riding just wasn't all that memorable. However, Dave and Bill and I did have a great trip and arrived back home with the satisfaction of having been part of it all.

Once back, I had to get busy as my intention was to travel back out to the west coast in just a few months to compete in no less than four nationals. I'd spent most of the $2,500 I'd gotten from Mr. No Name fixing up my old Chevy Suburban into a bike hauler/makeshift camper for me and my family as on this next trip I planned to take along my wife and all the kids. I'll be the first to admit that I'm the king of making due with what is available, with little to no consideration when it comes to aesthetics. And believe me, the Suburban camper was no looker. But that old 307-powered Chevy hauled us all the way back out to Saddleback Park, where the first national was to be held.

This time, the weather conditions were much more favorable as most all the sections were totally dry. I was riding decently, and the GRM was performing quite well. However, while riding hard between sections, the GRM seized. In an effort to get the bike to run as crisply as possible at low revs, I just had jetted it too lean. Well, as soon as the engine seized, I quickly pulled in the clutch and the rear tire stopped sliding, so I just let the bike coast along. Before coming to a complete stop, I popped the clutch, and the GRM fired right back up. Hoping for the best, I continued on at a more sedate pace. To my great relief, the bike continued running the rest of the day, and I was able to finish my ride.

The next event was the very next day, all the way up in Northern California. With no time to spare, we loaded up, and, with my wife driving, I pulled the bike apart in the back of the camper in an attempt to address what damage may have occurred to the engine. I got the top end apart and worked at hand-filing high spots off the piston. It certainly was a rudimentary repair, but with no replacement piston available, it would have to do.

We ended up driving straight through and fortunately made it to the next event in time. And amazingly, the GRM ran just fine all day. Following this event, we had a week free to actually enjoy some vacation time then headed to Oregon for the next national, held on Saturday, followed up by yet another national, in Washington State, on Sunday. To my great satisfaction, the GRM finished each one of them, and I enjoyed some terrific riding experiences in the greatly varied terrain each event presented.

Here it is—my famous, or infamous, homemade camper. Looking a bit worse for wear by the time this photo was taken, but in its time the old rig served us well. 307, and three-speed on the column. It got the job done!

These wonderful experiences were followed by many more aboard the GRM. There was no further communication between myself and Mr. No Name, however. I didn't go looking for him, and he never contacted me in regard to his motorcycle. The real tragedy in all this was, of course, the misfortune which befell Bill Grapevine, Charlie Hill, and various investors. Jim lost every dime which he had put into the effort, and Bill lost much more. All his time, effort, and certainly all his money were gone. My understanding was that the bank which financed Bill came after him full bore—tried taking everything from him, right down to his automobile. Interesting, considering that they allowed Mr. No Name to bamboozle them out of all the GRM assets without paying them anything. I must point out, however, that much of this is speculation on my part. I mean, these are not necessarily the absolute facts. Instead, it's just how the situation appeared from my perspective, and how things unfolded, to the best of my understanding and recollection.

Bill Grapevine claimed that there was a total of 250 GRM motorcycles produced. Jim Ellis told me that while that was possible, to his knowledge, there were only about one hundred which made their way into the original Wichita storage warehouse. So, maybe there are a bunch of GRMs running around to this day down in Mexico. Who knows? Bill Grapevine once told Jim Ellis that Moto Islo at one point sold off hundreds of GRMs in the Mexican market, which had been submerged in a flood. Here in the US, a GRM can still be occasionally spotted in the odd vintage trials event, and there are a few pictures floating around on the Internet. All in all, they are .a pretty obscure piece of equipment these days, for sure.

In the end, the GRM chapter of my life wrapped up rather uneventfully. I sold the first bike, the one which Bill Grapevine had originally given me to compete on, and it's my understanding that it ended up in a motorcycle junkyard. I did hold on to the second one for some time but eventually gave it to Bill Grapevine. It was not in all that good of shape and had simply been sitting around for years. I'd probably robbed some parts off it too. Becoming somewhat nostalgic as I've grown older, I recently approached Jim and asked if he had any GRMs in his possession, especially any which had remained complete and intact and, hopefully, in operational condition. To my surprise, Jim did indeed come up with, and sold to me, a very nice, all-original bike, which indeed runs. And so, my GRM experience has finally come full circle.

Looking back on it all, it is amazing to think about how Jim Ellis found his way to Candytown on that day in 1972 and chose to approach me of all people, with a proposal to ride the GRM. And then for me to take a chance on this obscure motorcycle, I never could have imagined the joy and satisfaction which eventually resulted. I've made my share of chancy decisions over the years, often at the drop of a hat, but this one turned out to be one of the best ever.

Addendum, by Jim Ellis: Although I personally contributed some eight thousand dollars to the GRM effort, I've always considered myself a personal friend to Bill Grapevine rather than just an investor. And despite the monies invested, and substantial efforts on my part to help Bill with the whole endeavor, neither do I consider myself as having been a "partner" in GRM. It was instead Charlie Hill, who was Bill's true partner. Charlie's association with Bill goes back to the time they both spent in the US Navy and later when they rode together in the 1950s. Plus, Charlie became a machinist and helped to finalize designs and create components from Bill's draw-ings. Charlie spent years working on various projects with Bill, made many trips to Mexico with Bill to coordinate with Carabella and later Moto Islo, and later went on the road with his old friend, working to convince dealers to carry GRMs.

With Bill based in Wichita, and me having moved out to the East coast, there were times when I didn't see him for years. Plus, I never was involved with any of the negotiations or agreements with Carabella and Moto Islo. Or was I part of Bill's arrangements with the Wichita bank, which provided the means to actually get the GRMs into production. I was, of course, very curious about all that was going on during that time period. I wrote a lot of letters to Bill and would occasionally receive a response. I did purchase and take possession of one of the first twenty-five GRMs produced and con-stantly tinkered with it, trying to come up with ideas which could possibly help Bill to improve later versions of the bike. And I did "discover" Jerry Young, helped to get him set up with a GRM, and eventually traveled to various venues to photograph Jerry, all with intentions to help sell the bikes. But I never was a part of the GRM "business" and, as a result, was never contacted by the Wichita bank when they eventually began to try to recover their investment.

You could say that I "bought into Bill's dream." Those were exciting times, and I was really caught up in all of it. Plus, such was my friendship with Bill that I helped him out financially for years after GRM was history. I also worked with Bill on his ten "Past Masters" trials events and rode in every one of them.

Jerry rode them all too. Together with Jerry and his son, Mike, I attended Bill's funeral, which if I recall correctly, was in January of 2004. I presented Bill's eulogy that day, and Jerry spoke briefly. Jerry and I were pallbearers at the funeral as well. That day was the last time I saw Charlie Hill too. In the wake of Bill's passing, we simply lost touch.

In the end, I guess you could say that Bill Grapevine was one of my favorite people, a man who wholeheartedly pursued his dreams and saw them through to reality.

I once managed to visit the Wichita GRM warehouse facility after the bank had locked the place up and peeked in through a window. Inside, I spotted about half a dozen of those Stiletto kick-start levers, suggesting that Bill had installed the rest of them on bikes, which would in turn points to some one hundred bikes possibly having been sold. Yes, the GRM motorcycle was not a sound design, and, yes, the company did go bankrupt. Regardless, I still feel very fortunate to have been involved in what was a great adventure.

CHAPTER 8

Young Enterprises

My own shop!

I must plead to some uncertainty of the exact point in time when I established my own trials shop. It was nearly forty years prior to my sitting here and writing down these recollections. And, to be honest, I have not retained all the records and documentation from that period in my life. However, by my best estimation, it was 1981, so we'll go with that.

So, 1981, and I'm deep into trials, am raising a big family, and several of my offspring want to ride. I'm just a poor working man, so opening up a shop seemed a logical way to combine my interests and needs and supplement my income. Back then, it was a fairly simple process to become a dealer, at least when it came to brands with limited distribution in the United States. I began with Montesa, which was at the time handled by Larry Wise of Cosmopolitan Motors, located right over in eastern Pennsylvania. Two bikes (one of which was for me), some parts, and I was in business.

I set up shop in the basement of my home, and with my established connections in the local and regional observed trials community, I actually did pretty well. I brought in a bunch of boots and tires, stocked some shelves with parts, and worked on all kinds of bikes. And that was a very busy time for me—working all day at my job, then once finally home, filling a bunch of parts orders to be shipped, and turning wrenches. Plus, during this same time, I was still competing in trials, hosting local trials events, and laying the groundwork for my (mine and PTR, that is) National Observed Trials event.

Promotion of my shop, my trials events, and observed trials in general was a very important part of everything I was hoping to accomplish, so considerable effort was made in that area. I conducted trails training classes on my own property, including bicycle trials, which at that time was receiving a considerable amount of attention. We put on a lot of demonstrations too. At locations such as Cosmopolitan Motors' facility, we would set up man-made obstacles, and even little trials sections, and provide the general public with an idea of what trials is all about.

We conducted a number of Trials demonstrations to promote not only my business, but also the sport in general. Check out the sign you can just see through my Montesa's front spokes—"Motorcycle Skill Riding".

Another one of our promotional efforts. Check out
Ryan's trials bicycle in the background.

Such demos were also set up at the Lycoming Mall, nearby to my home in Williamsport, where we climbed around on a VW Beetle and even rode over some obstacles inside the mall! PTR was there as well, with a little trials section we'd set up, with hauled-in rocks and logs. We even managed to set up a demo at the Jacob Javits Center in New York City as well as at an event in Baltimore.

Daughter Laura Lee, helping to promote the business.

In addition to the business I generated simply as the result of being a well-known figure in local and regional trials, I also advertised in *Feet Up* magazine—a publication dedicated to the sport of observed trials. Plus, my overall involvement and activities eventually led to a regular column in *Feet Up*, which I called "Because I Care." The articles I wrote featured my take on the sport of observed trials. And with great respect for Larry Wise, owner of Cosmopolitan Motors, such was my involvement with all the above described efforts and activities; people at the time seemed to have the impression that I was the eastern distributor for the observed trials market, not just a dealer.

And the business "thrived." I say it that way because while a lot of money passed through my hands, not a whole lot necessarily stayed in my pocket. I approached, and conducted, my little business the same way as every effort I've made my entire life—with the utmost of professionalism and drive for success. And that's no general statement, either. I really mean what those words represent. It's been difficult to express in this book what kind of effort and drive I put into everything I've even done without sounding boastful or full of myself. And yet this is who I am and, quite frankly, how I've managed to accomplish and achieve all that I have.

So, back to the business, we did okay. Later on, I added the Beta brand to the "line" of bikes I offered and even hired a girl to answer the phone during the day. And yet there was that money thing, significant revenue but not a whole lot of profit. Considering the amount of effort I was putting forth, in the end, the resulting financial yield just did not justify continuing. I wrapped things up right around 1992, the year I rode the Scottish Six Days Trial.

I like to think my efforts helped to establish a presence by the Beta company in the U.S. market. They certainly were, and are, fine bikes. I'm mounted on a 250 in this picture, and needed just a little assistance in this particularly challenging section.

Flyin' high. This is an earlier, air-cooled version of the little 125 Beta we sold.

These were promo shots for Young's Enterprise advertisements.

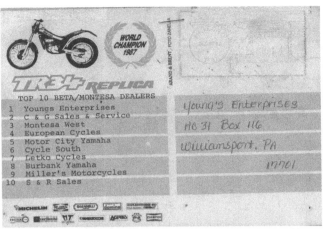

Young's Enterprises—sounds like an investment firm or something, doesn't, it? Regardless, there we are—number one Beta dealer in the U.S., in 1987.

It is important to note that I owe a great deal to Larry Wise of Cosmopolitan Motors. Larry was a great friend and ally during my time as a motorcycle dealer and is a story unto himself. Larry's business, Cosmopolitan Motors, goes back to his grandfather, who was a distributor of Singer products in the family's native, Hungary. Larry's father emigrated to the US in 1922, at which time he founded Cosmopolitan Motors and, based in New York City, began importing Jawa/CZ. Larry joined the company when he came of age and eventually took over when his father retired. Cosmopolitan continually expanded the number of brands they imported into the US, including Parilla, Zundapp, Benilli, and Ducati, among others. A key employee early on was Joe Berliner, who in time went out on his own and established Berliner Motor Corporation.

After Joe's departure, Larry relocated Cosmo to Germantown, Pennsylvania, near Philadelphia, where operations continued, expanding to include Montesa and eventually Beta. And with these brands in particular, Larry not only served as importer but, in my opinion, also kept the sport of observed trials going in the United States. Larry regularly hosted race teams from the factories for US events and, like me, conducted many promotional events. Larry also sponsored his own observed trials team, with the Beta brand, and I was fortunate enough to be among his selected riders.

Larry was also a tremendous mentor to my son, Ryan, beginning when Ryan was so young that Larry would have to hold him up on the motorcycle until Ryan could get the bike moving. Larry's support of Ryan went well beyond that of sponsor, at times arranging for Ryan to be transported to trials events in a limousine so that Ryan would be fresh and well-rested when he arrived. Even when Ryan was still quite young, Larry in fact predicted that Ryan would become national champion.

At the time this book is being written, Larry Wise is eighty-nine years of age, still going strong, and in fact is still running Cosmopolitan Motors. Admittedly, Larry has, after all these years, finally begun to wind things down, however. He is presently selling off his inventory and looking to close the business and retire.

After all his years in business, all the terrific motorcycles he has brought into this country, and all his contributions to our sport, I think Larry has earned his retirement. He sure helped me. I'll never forget all that he did for me and for Ryan and how much he helped me with Young Enterprises.

We had a great time participating each year in the local Mummers Parade, popping wheelies and doing stoppies all along the parade route. It was an excellent way to promote Young's Enterprises to the local community, too. We even had a "section" built on top of a trailer, pulled behind my Suburban, enabling our riders to hop aboard and perform brief but interesting demonstrations.

CHAPTER 9

The Scottish Six Days Trial

My ultimate goal, realized.

I'd long been intent on riding the Scottish Six Days Trial. First held in 1909, the "Scottish" is one of the world's oldest motorsports events and, in my mind, the ultimate goal for any trials rider. My many other obligations, however, prevented me from fulfilling this promise to myself for many years. In fact, it was not until after I had hosted many, many local events, multiple national events, two international trials, and had served as president of PTR for many years did I finally find time to dedicate myself to such a major endeavor on my own behalf.

Finally, in the fall of 1990, I began discussing the matter with my wife. Fortunately, Kelley was all for it and simply told me, "You'd better do it before you get too old!" So, here I was, at fifty years of age, making plans to participate in what is quite likely the toughest observed trials event in the world. The thing was, regardless of my age, I had no doubts whatsoever about being up to the challenge. Not that I considered myself to be a superman or anything, it's just I was in shape, had been riding consistently for years, and was confident in my abilities. Still, six days on the pegs of a trials bike, riding approximately one hundred miles per day, and tackling some thirty scored sections during each of those days is a challenge not to be taken lightly.

There were a considerable number of details to address in the months leading up to the 1991 event, not the least of which was to submit a request to participate. That's right. You didn't just sign up to ride the Scottish Trial. Instead, there was an application which must be submitted, along with a description of the rider's experience, level of skill, and other details. Then, of course, there were the basics, such as securing a passport, acquiring airline tickets, and arranging for lodging while in Scotland. Also, a big decision was whether to ship my own bike over or rent one in Scotland to use during the event. Fortunately, I found out that John Lampkin rented bikes to ride in the Scottish, and even though the cost was considerable, two thousand dollars back in 1991, the convenience and security of having a bike all set up and ready to ride far outweighed the complexities and uncertainties of trying to get my own bike packed up and shipped over there. Interestingly, I later found that after the rental bikes like mine were ridden for the one week of the event, John Lampkin simply sold them as slightly used machines, Scottish Six Days proven too.

I felt little anxiety as the time drew close for my May departure. Everything was in place, such as travel arrangements, lodging, and the rental bike. Plus, although I would be traveling alone, there were to be friends and associates present at the Scottish, with some participating in the event along with me. For example, I had found out through the grapevine that a fellow with whom I'd ridden multiple events, Bill DeGaris from Vancouver, British Columbia, was also going to ride the 1991 event. Also, although I didn't know it at the time, Bob Howard, the fellow who in later years expressed how I had been a role model for him, was also to be there. It wasn't until I had arrived in Scotland that I encountered Bob and realized he was set up to ride that year as well.

Bill DeGaris and I, in a relaxed moment. Believe this would have been in the morning, before heading out. Photo credit: Mike Dunfree

In addition to these fellow riders, two other individuals whom I'd come to know where going to be at the event, Norm "Wick" Wicker and his wife, Marilyn. Marilyn and Wick are two of the most wonderful people I have met in my entire life. Wick was an airline pilot by trade, and he and Marilyn attended the Scottish every year, not to compete, but simply to be there, to enjoy the spectacle of the event, and to help out. Wick typically volunteered to be a "judge" during the event, their term for a checker. Plus, Wick and Marilyn served as the go-to people for American riders interested in riding the Scottish. They were, in fact, extremely helpful in assisting me to organize all the details required for my trip to the event. And as if all that was not enough, throughout each year, Marilyn conducted fundraisers, the proceeds of which were used to help fund US riders to attend and compete in the Scottish. I very much regret that time and circumstances resulted in me losing touch with Wick and Marilyn. Two very special people among the best in the sport ever.

Hand-stitched by Marilyn Wicker. "HaadForrit" is the Scottish term for the Trial.

Another acquaintance who attended the 1991 event was Mike Dunfree, a fellow Pennsylvania resident who was there to spectate and to take photographs. It is Mike to whom I am so very grateful for providing the pictures which accompany this chapter.

As a brief overview of the Scottish Six Days Trial, the event was, as I've mentioned, first run in 1909! Hosted since its inception by the Edinburgh Motor Club, the event was, until 1977, held near to the city of Edinburgh. Post-'77, however, the trials has been run out of Fort William, Scotland, which is located in the western Scottish Highlands, on the shores of Loch Linnhe, itself not far from the Atlantic Ocean. It's a mountainous area, very rugged, with lots of rocks, and filled with the area's famous "moors," which is basically an area of open meadows and muddy bogs, with no trees, just low, scrubby vegetation. The Scottish is held early in the month of May, and considering how far north Scotland is in general, and Fort William is in particular, that means the weather can be quite cold—and wet! The trials runs for six days, of course, beginning Monday and completing on Saturday. Each day's loop consists of about 100 miles of riding and includes many "judged" sections per day. So, combined with the length of the event, distance per day, rugged terrain, and challenging weather, it is for sure one tough ride.

And so, early in the month of May, 1991, I boarded a plane for Edinburgh, Scotland, and once there rode a train across the northern part of the country and eventually arrived in Fort William. The place was really hopping, as the Scottish is certainly a very big deal, with plenty of people in attendance. Fortunately, I was set up right in town, at the Fort William Hotel, and had no problem checking in and getting settled. The next day, Sunday, I located John Lampkin and assured my rental bike was there and ready to go. John had me set up with a brand-new, '91 Beta 250 Trials, and since I was at that time riding a Beta trials back home, I felt very comfortable on the bike. Just the same, I put on my gear and took a ride on the Beta, as the organizers had set up an area just down the road for us to do a little riding before the event, just to get a bit acclimated. I also got myself registered, of course, and ran the bike through tech inspection. All went well, and the bike was then secured in the Pare Ferme as, per SSDT rules, all competitors' machines were sequestered every night.

I also wandered around a bit, simply taking in the atmosphere of the event. It was definitely exciting, what with riders from all over the world present, bikes being ridden everywhere, rows of vendors set up, and all of it taking place right in and around the town of Fort William. There was no need in fact to haul the bikes anywhere as each day's start took place literally walking distance from my hotel.

Good thing those vendors were on hand because I ended up purchasing a riding jacket for myself before the start of the event. You see, I had brought along all my riding gear, which was adequate for the conditions back home in Pennsylvania—one pair each of boots, riding pants, gloves, and my helmet and for the bike, just a couple of spare plugs and a handful of tools. So, I got there and saw just how cold it was and figured that I absolutely was going to need a jacket. Well, I located a decent jacket from among the vendors, one which supposed to be waterproof (turned out it wasn't) and figured I was now ready to go!

With everything now in place, there was only one concern nagging at me. I was injured, you see. It happened a week prior to the event. I was at home and decided to take my bike down the road a piece from my residence, where I've got a little riding section laid out. It was a fine day, and I was feeling pretty full of myself, all set and ready to go ride the Scottish Six Days in just a week's time. So, I'm doing this nice wheelie down the pavement, and all of a sudden, I lose it, and the bike loops over backward. Well, I kicked the Beta away and landed on my feet—doing about 25 miles per hour. I took about two or three gigantic, long strides before the momentum overcame my efforts to stay upright and went tumbling up the road. Got up, dusted myself off, and took stock of the situation. No apparent injuries from the tumble, as I had all my gear on, but one foot in particular was really hurting. Apparently, I'd bruised my heel pretty badly during one of those six-foot strides. I didn't go to the doctor, just sucked it up, hoping the injury wouldn't cause any problems for me during the six days' ride. I actually tried devising some sort of arrangement on my own Beta, which would allow me to rest the injured foot while riding down road sections at the Scottish, figuring I could then transfer the setup to the rental bike. In the end though I gave up on the idea and decided I was just going to have to tough it out. Six days on the pegs. Oh, boy. What a way to start what was to be one of the greatest adventures of my life.

Despite hobbling around a bit, favoring that injured foot, came Monday morning, and I was ready to go! I was so very excited and just felt great. The photos taken of me during the week may not necessarily convey my happiness, but I had an ear-to-ear grin virtually every moment I was in Scotland. My room at the hotel was warm and comfy, I'd slept well, had been enjoying some great food, and now I was ready to climb aboard my brand-new rental bike, about to head out and tackle whatever the event had in store for me.

I was so very excited to be a part of the Scottish Six-Days Trial. Every moment of every day was an absolute thrill. I will never forget it. What a great experience.

The start area was literally walking distance from my hotel, so after breakfast, I geared up, collected my bike out of the Pare Ferme, and pushed it into line behind the riders who were starting ahead of me. I had been assigned riding number 151, which suited me just fine for the first day. It meant that I'd have a pretty clear trail to follow as I had no idea where we were going. To my best recollection, we had no route charts, relying instead on following arrows to direct us down the road sections and along the trails. Covering one hundred miles per day, plus negotiating all the judged sections, all within the prescribed time limit, meant we had to hustle down the road sections pretty much just as fast as the bikes would go. I definitely remember holding the Beta nearly wide open in top gear, pretty regularly, so staying on course was no easy matter.

So, what was it like riding the course? Well, nothing I wasn't prepared for but tough, no doubt. Lots of rocks, some water, and some mud, too, but not terribly mucky or anything like that. I was fortunate to some extent as everyone was talking about how '91 was a "relatively dry year." We had some rain during the week, and it was definitely cool the entire time we were there, but it is my understanding that the Scottish is often a very wet affair, and cold, with much more rain and much wetter conditions than what I experienced. Generally speaking, the main difference by comparison to all the other trials events I'd ridden up that point was the daily mileage. Getting one hundred or so miles in each day meant that we not only had to really haul ass down the road sections but it also meant that there was a limit to the time available to walk sections prior to riding them. Plus, the sections were really long, typically three judges in each one. There were plenty of times when I would walk just the first part of sections then just wing it from there.

We were frequently confronted with rocky creek beds such as this one. Note other riders checking my lines, plus marshals watching for dabs.

Despite all this, throughout that first day, I was doing quite well. The bike was working great, I hadn't gotten lost, crashed, or ran into any real problems. Plus, I was riding smart, taking threes as was necessary, and focusing on pacing myself. After all, there were five more days ahead of us. Still, always in the back of mind was getting one hundred miles in and not breaking out of the daily time limit. So, late in the day, I'm flying down one of those road sections, looking forward to finishing up. Up ahead I see a checkpoint and wouldn't you know, there's my buddy, Wick, ready to mark my card. A friendly face to welcome me to the finish! When I handed my card over, however, Wick looked at it and said, "Jerry, you missed a checkpoint!"

I was dumbfounded for a moment or two. How could I have missed a checkpoint? My mind raced. Didn't seem like I'd gotten off course at all. Maybe at one point when I was flying down the road, passing cars and all, possibly I flew right by it. Wick indicated the one I missed was the next-to-last checkpoint, so with no idea how the rules applied with such a situation and, in my mind, no alternative, I spun around and hauled back in the direction I'd just come. Sure enough, some miles back up the road, there was the checkpoint I'd missed. And if the crew there happened to notice that I'd come flying in from the wrong direction, nobody said anything about it, and I sure wasn't going to volunteer anything. They simply marked my card, and I took off down the road once again heading back to the final checkpoint, hoping against hope that my screwup didn't result in disqualification. None too soon the final checkpoint appeared once again, and to my great relief, Wick indicated that I'd made it in under the time limit. I was relieved and happy and all in all was quite pleased with myself. It had been a good ride, and I now had day one of the Scottish Six Days Trial under my belt. I had two things on my mind at that point, a hot bath and some food. It had indeed been quite cool all day; I was plenty wet, and I hadn't had anything to eat since breakfast.

That hot bath surely did feel good, and a hearty meal afterward was equally as satisfying. After dinner, I got the chance to meet some of guys responsible for laying out the course. I commented to these fellows about how impressed I was that they were able to put together one hundred miles loops for each day, each one filled with substantial off-road sections. Considering my own experience in securing land use for off-road events, I was curious about how they managed to do so for an event the size and extent of the Scottish. These fellows were big, rugged guys, with full beards, ruddy cheeks, and big, calloused hands. They looked for all the world like lumberjacks. We talked for a while, and they described how negotiations with virtually every landowner involved bottles of whiskey, and in each case, they wouldn't leave the discussion until the whiskey was gone and access to the land secured.

Next day, I was up early and ready to go but definitely feeling stiff and sore. All my riding gear, especially my boots, was still plenty wet, but I had no choice. So, into my one set of gear and back to the Pare Ferme to collect my bike. Can't say that I performed any particular maintenance on the bike, just the basic stuff—checked tire pressure, chain tension, made sure nothing was ready to fall off, and on to tech inspection. Yes, the organizers checked the bikes every day before turning us loose. Very thoroughly too. Guess they did want us going out there and hurting ourselves—at least not as the result of a detectable issue with the bike. The tires on my Beta held up well all week, and I never felt the need to change either one of them. I experienced no flats throughout the event either. Good thing, too, as I had no spare tubes with me and certainly no replacement tires. Should there have been need for a tire, or a tube, I suppose I would have had to buy them. Interestingly, one of the details the tech guys looked for every day was missing knobs off the tires. Would there been any absent, the rider was required to change the tire before heading out on the course. Lucky for me, the knobs on my tires all stayed put all week.

Heading out then on day two, I at least had some idea of what to expect from the course, how fast I had to ride the road sections, and how much time I could take in each judged section. And the bottom line was that there was no time to be dilly-dallying around. The time schedule, the course, and the event in general did in fact result in riders in DNF as the result of houring out. The Scottish was definitely not for amateurs!

It's difficult to tell in the picture, but this is one steep climb. Lots of spectators present here, too, unlike other parts of the course where the riders were out there all alone. Photo credit: Mike Dunfree

Regardless, I maintained the outlook of focusing on one section at a time, not worrying about what lay ahead or what we were to encounter on subsequent days. Each of us were pretty much on our own too. I did not ride with a "group" any time during the week. The course was so long, and with each rider focused on maintaining his own schedule, about the only time I saw other riders was when someone faster would overtake me on a road section or when waiting to ride a judged section. I cannot overemphasize that it was quite scary on the road sections. These were open roadways, with traffic in both directions, quite mountainous, plus we were riding on the left (British traffic laws) side of the road. Very fast riding, in top gear, was generally required, which definitely required maximum focus at all times. Not too fast, however, as it was necessary to preserve the bike in order for it to last the entire week. Quite challenging to balance the two.

Tuesday turned out to be another good day for me. I kept my cool, hammered the road sections, used common sense in the judged sections, and as a result didn't crash, didn't hour out, and finished up feeling pretty good. Ditto for Wednesday. Thursday, however, held an additional challenge for me. Remember my starting number of 151? Well, the riders started each day in order by their number, except that the schedule rotated forward each day in increments of fifty. So, day one, rider number one was first out. Day two, rider number fifty-one left first. Day three, 101. Got it? So that meant, yep, old Jerry was first rider out on day four, Thursday. And I had no idea where I was going, so I immediately let some numbers behind me go by to forge the trail.

Still, with only a handful of riders ahead of me, the trail was nowhere nearly as well worn-in as had been on the first three days when many, many riders started ahead of me. As a result, I took a few bad lines. One in particular involved this innocent-looking little pool of water. I could see the trail on the other side of it and, suspecting nothing treacherous, rode right into the pool. Well, my Beta just nosed right in, the front wheel completely disappearing into deep mud under the shallow pool of water. I got myself extracted from the muck, but there was no way I was going to get the bike out of there under my own power. In mere moments, however, another rider approached, stopped and came right over, and helped me get the Beta back onto solid ground. The rider was none other than eventual winner of the event, Steve Saunders. I thanked him profusely, but Steve just shrugged it off and said cheerily, in his classic British accent, "No worries! You can help me later!"

An early morning shot, and we're all enjoying a sunny day. Coming up out of that creek bottom in the background. This is the first part of a typically long section. Photo credit: Mike Dunfree

There's a dab. A quite challenging section. Look at those rocks! I've gotten off line a little bit, and still have a long way to go. Check the rider in the upper right-hand corner, looking for his line even further along. The marker flags can be seen too. Photo credit: Mike Dunfree

Yet another challenge occurred later that same day when, while crossing a big, open field, the flags we'd been following simply disappeared. Remember that in the "moors" of Scotland, there are virtually no trees on which to staple arrows. Instead, the course is often marked with little flags on wire rods, simply pushed into the soft ground. Well, all indications pointed to some joker riding, or walking, along and pulling out the flags as they went. With few riders ahead of me that day, there was a considerable amount time spent literally riding around and looking for the course or more flags to indicate where we were supposed to go. And all during this time, I was, of course, worried about houring out. More riders arrived in the area, and we all spread out, trying to pick up the course. Fortunately, we finally found our way and were once more back on track. I don't remember how much time I lost, but it was certainly more than I, or any of the other riders, should have. What a shame that some inconsiderate people would jeopardize the efforts of riders in such a prestigious event. For many entrants such as myself, this was a once-in-a-lifetime experience. Imagine all that time, money, and effort invested only to be undone by some idiots sabotaging the course.

Despite that one disappointment, I could not have been happier with the course, the riding, and the event in general. After all, here I was, participating in the most important observed trials event in the world, in Scotland, against the very best riders in the sport. What could be better? By any measure, the Scottish was indeed a spectacular experience. The scope and history of the event, being a part of something that so many people aspire to, it was everything I could have hoped for. I looked forward to every single one of the six days of riding. Everyone was great! One day, I forgot that we actually rode to a ferry crossing and were transported to an island and rode sections there! It was terrific!

And so, it went. Day after day, I wheeled my bike out each morning and, in the allotted ten-minute grace period, checked over the Beta and headed out on my minute. The bike ended up running perfectly all week, requiring nothing other than to assure all was in order each clay. No flats and no breakdowns. I may have adjusted the chain a bit, but that's it. As for myself, I felt great all week. Oh, I was tired and sore, of course, and was in no way a fan of climbing into cold, wet gear every morning, but I was so thrilled and happy to be there, riding this fantastic event that none of the slight discomfort mattered. The weather was not all that bad. It was cool and did rain on us off and on all week but no torrential downpours or anything like that.

One thing for sure about Scotland—it's wet! Check out all the moss on the ground and on the trees. Photo credit: Mike Dunfree

Ah, but all too soon the sixth day arrived. It was another great day, but then I was done. It hit the final check, and that was it. No waving checkered flags, no cheering throngs of spectators. No, we were just done. There was a final tech inspection to "my" Beta to assure none of the sealed parts had been tampered with, and once cleared, I had officially completed the Scottish. I turned in the bike and walked back to the hotel for the last time.

Saturday night was the awards banquet, at which time I was very pleased to find I had finished 197th overall, having amassed 569 points. Not bad for my first try against the best riders in the world, many of whom were half my age. Steve Saunders, the overall winner, dropped just 35 points in six days of riding. Wow!

Receiving my award for six days of intense riding. Note
my PTR-logoed shirt. Photo credit: Mike Dunfree

After what definitely ranks as one of the best experiences of
my life, it was finally time to head home. My buddy from British
Columbia, Billy DeGaris, and I rented a car and drove down to
London. There, we enjoyed a few touristy experiences, then it was
back to the US. Once home, I couldn't say that I went around brag-
ging about how I had ridden the Scottish Six Days Trial, and none
of my friends came banging down my door wanting to know all
about it. No, it was more of a personal success and achievement, and
I continuously thank myself for having put forth the time and effort
to make it happen. In my mind, there is no doubt, the Scottish definitely is the greatest trials event in the world.

CHAPTER 10

Past Masters

Bill Grapevine's Legacy

Long after the demise of his ill-fated GRM motorcycle venture, my old friend, Bill Grapevine, put together a series of observed trials events out in Kansas, which he called Past Masters. To be more specific, Bill called his events the Past Master Vintage Trials, with the intent of bringing together veteran riders from all over to compete aboard noncurrent trails machinery.

The Wichita Eagle

Mike Hutmacher/The Wichita Eagle

Motorcycle builder and racer Bill Grapevine displays his 1967 national champion trophy and a replica of his 1962 GRM Maverick off-road trial cycle.

Excerpt from an article Jim Ellis wrote about Bill, which was published in a Kansas newspaper.

The first one took place in 1992, and after hearing about it through Jim Ellis, I made plans to head out there and participate. Bill set up the course at a place called Rocky Ridge Resort, out in Fradonia, Kansas, near to Bill's home base in Leon, Kansas, and I was anxious not only to ride the event but to reunite with Bill. He'd had some serious health problems in the years since I'd seen him last, and neither of us were getting any younger.

Before getting into the event itself, I must share an interesting story about our trip out to Kansas that year, which was not without some challenges. You will recall how I've explained that I never had a whole whopping bunch of money to work with, so means of travel and transport for myself and my motorcycles to various parts of the country were always quite modest. Well, this time was to be different, or so I thought.

My friend, Dick Oliver, had signed on to go with me out to Bill's first event, and we were to be traveling in style, courtesy of a thirty-three-foot motorhome I had acquired. With the bikes on a trailer behind us, Dick and I had plenty of room up front and all the comforts of home. Not to mention, we'd be all set for camping once we got out to Kansas. All was fine until right smack in the middle of a bridge spanning the Mississippi River, this horrible rapping sound came up through the "doghouse" inside the motorhome beneath which was located the engine and transmission. Fortunately, we managed to limp the rest of the way across the bridge, found a place to pull off, and tried to figure out what was going on.

An initial assessment revealed some bad news. It looked as though the RV's transmission was trying to separate itself from the engine! Dick thought at first that a weld job might be all that was needed, so we managed to drive the rig a bit further to a shop, where we hoped to make repairs. Further investigation though showed more serious issues. Before it was all said and done, and after working all night with a young man at the shop where we were stranded, we had gutted another transmission which matched the one in our rig, mixed and matched housings and parts, bolted everything up, and we were back in business. After more than twenty-four hours, between driving and repairing the RV, we pulled in to Bill's event.

So, Bill had set up Past Masters as a two-day event, with some fifty sections each day. The course was really impressive, with lots of rocks and streams and gullies to challenge the riders. The venue was really nice too. Rocky Ridge Resort was quite nice, with a restaurant on-site, cabins to rent, and just a beautiful layout. There was a very good turnout for Bill's first effort, maybe forty riders, most of them veterans like myself and Dick. I had entered my Cub that year, rode the expert class, and won it. Bill took good care of us too. He had commemorative T-shirts, a beautiful event program, which ran between twenty-four and thirty-six pages, and terrific course maps like the one shown in this chapter—penned by Bill himself! Plus, the awards were awesome: medals and oak plaques and, for the top scorers, silver-plated bows and cups on walnut pedestals. Plus, we all enjoyed a wonderful banquet on Saturday night.

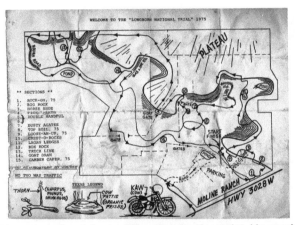

Among his many other talents, Bill was quite the artist. He would sketch up course layout diagrams such as this one for the Past Masters events.

Everyone who attended that first Past Masters really enjoyed it, and word spread quickly that Bill had hosted an absolutely top-notch event. There was much anticipation then for a repeat of the event, and Bill did not disappoint. He in fact did a good bit of marketing to work on attracting some of the biggest names in the sport. In all, Bill held ten Past Masters events, and I am pleased to say that I participated in every one of them. In fact, thanks to Bill, I was treated like a bit of a celebrity each year when I was out there. And that's really saying something because over the years, there were a lot of more prominent riders than me competing at the Past Masters. My son, Ryan Young, multi-time National Observed Trials Champion, National Champ Curt Comer, and World Champion Mike Andrews were just a few of the "big names" who made the trip to Kansas various years to ride with us.

Speaking of how well Bill treated me at his events, one year I was hoping to ride out there on my street bike and asked Bill if he could supply me with a trials machine on which to compete. Bill said that would be no problem at all, so I made the trip out from Pennsylvania on my Honda CBX1000, riding all night and arriving just in time for the riders meeting on Saturday morning. That ended up being a 2,300-mile round trip, which I used as a "practice ride" for my next excursion on the CBX—all the way to Alaska and back. You might say that I've "earned my chops" as a road rider as well as in the sport of observed trials.

As if he had not already accomplished enough in his life, Bill really shined with the Past Masters events. These truly were wonderful experiences for everyone fortunate enough to have been involved and were an absolute testament to the drive and dedication that Bill Grapevine possessed, not to mention his total commitment to the sport of motorcycling. Consider, for example, that Bill was already sixty-one years of age when he started the Past Masters and continued hosting them for another ten years! Also, and many people don't know this, Bill suffered a terrible injury some seven years into his efforts with the Past Masters yet recovered and continued on. Such was the nature of Bill's injury, and the fact that he managed to recover and continue on, make the details worth mentioning here.

That's Bill, me, my son Mike, and Jim Ellis, at the conclusion of one of Bill's Past Masters events. We're standing behind one of Bill's original, hard-tail GRM's, and it appears Mike and Jim and I have all come away with awards.

Remember first that Bill had gone through some very serious medical problems before even launching the Past Masters to the extent that most people suffering similar issues would have likely about given up entirely. Bill, however, put that all behind him and focused on producing a world-class series of observed trials events, such that any club or organization would be proud to lay claim to. But then some seven years into his efforts, Bill was out working on the course one evening, all alone, when he hit a hole on the trail and was tossed over the bars. While he wasn't knocked out, Bill realized that he couldn't move. His arms, legs, hands, nothing would work. No one knew where he was at the time, so there was no prospect of anyone necessarily coming to look for him. Lying there on the trail, Bill could hardly even call out for help. However, he eventually heard some sounds, which turned out to be two young girls paddling a canoe down the nearby river. The girls quite fortunately heard Bill's weak cries and, after finding him, called for an ambulance. Once in the hospital, it was discovered that Bill had broken his neck!

So, here's this man, nearly seventy years of age, having already fought back from cancer, lying in the hospital with a broken neck.

This same man, my very good friend, not only recovered from that terrible injury, but, as soon as he could, got right back to work on his event. And that was what made people like Bill Grapevine the true heroes of our sport—those who gave virtually their entire lives over to providing for the enjoyment of others, all so that we may experience the joy of having fun on two wheels.

CHAPTER 11

Ryan Young

In My Footsteps

It is very difficult, as the father of seven children, to highlight just one of them for a detailed story. Each of my kids are very special, I love them all dearly, and every single one possesses admirable talents and have each succeeded in their own way. However, considering the nature of this book, it is Ryan Young about whom we will talk about here.

Motorcycles are, of course, an integral part of our family, and all the kids at one time or another were riding about on two wheels. In fact, early on, the oldest ones kept my little Cub extremely well-used as they rode it literally every single day during the summer months while I was at work. Eventually, however, it was Mike and Ryan who stuck with it, began riding trials, and advanced up through the classes to reach the expert level.

Success in any endeavor requires, of course, a tremendous amount of time, effort, dedication, and skill. This is especially true in any type of sports competition, where an individual is challenged by the efforts of many other like-minded individuals. As such, it is absolutely necessary to focus extensively on the ultimate goal, often at the expense of a "typical" lifestyle. As a result, there are many individuals out there who possess tremendous skills in any one capacity yet who opt to go the path most of us do—pursuing a career, raising a family, etc. Such is the case with my son, Mike. Older than Ryan by three years, by the time he was in his teens, Mike was riding trials regularly, had achieved the level of expert, and was, and is, an extremely skilled rider. At the age of eighteen though, Mike made the decision to join the military, later married, raised a family, and has done quite well for himself. Through his commitments to his career and family, Mike was away from the sport for twenty-three years. Such are his skills, however, that upon returning to riding, Mike picked right up where he left off and does just as well in trials competition as when he was a teenager.

All of my kids were involved with Trials at one time or another, but it was Mike and Ryan who participated the most, even when they were just youngsters. That's Mike on the right, and Ryan on my left. Behind us, in bib overalls, is Lane Levitt. Over my left shoulder, and unfortunately all but hidden from view, is Debbie Evans.

Ryan, by comparison, is the one who stuck with it. Through his teen years, and beyond, Ryan continued a severe regimen of riding, training, competition, and dedication to the sport. These efforts, and much more, led to Ryan earning six consecutive National Observed Trials Championships. This level of achievement, at the national level, in any type of competition is astounding. Consider that there are many, many extremely skilled and dedicated individuals who, despite every effort they can possibly muster and despite considerable success in their chosen sport, never do succeed in earning a national title. And yet Ryan managed to earn six titles in a row. To this day, I still can barely comprehend what he achieved.

So, how did he get there? Well, as I've indicated, all the kids were riding bikes early on. They rode my Cub, and then there was a gaggle of Yamaha TY80s we had at one time, each of which were ridden virtually to death. Ryan, however, began competing in trials before he himself could even ride a motorcycle. How? Crazy as it may sound in today's world of extensive parental concern and control, and what with liability issues crippling virtually all activities these days, back then I had Ryan riding trials with me at three or four years of age. Yep. Had him sitting on the bike in front of me, holding on to the bars, with me up on the pegs riding sections. He loved it, too, and just as soon as he was big enough, Ryan got on one of those TY80s.

As his skills developed, Ryan and I began training together quite seriously. We would ride the practice sections I have laid out on my own property every night after I got home from work. And this was summer and winter too. Ryan will tell you about going out and clearing snow off the sections so he could ride them. We'd be out there in all weather conditions—sunshine, rain, snow, you name it.

These champions are a family affair

Jerry Young leads his son, Ryan, over some of the "easy" terrain they encounter in motorcycle trials competition.   These champions keep their success all in the family. Fo more, please turn to Page B12.

Ryan and I, featured in yet another newspaper article.

Ryan started out in the novice class, of course, but it did not take him long to progress through intermediate, and amateur, and then on to expert—at the age of thirteen! We rode all the local events, but then Ryan began traveling with me to out-of-state competitions as well, all the time developing his skill and capabilities. And it wasn't just on the motorcycles or even in observed trials riding that Ryan demonstrated special capabilities. I have been told that in school, for example, Ryan would show off by doing handstands on top of desks. Not only handstands in fact, but he reportedly could perform handstand push-ups. That was he'd be doing a full handstand up on top of a school desk, lever his arms down until he could touch his chin on the desktop, then extend his arms back up again! Also, at one point in time, we ended up with a unicycle at the house. Ryan not only became very proficient on that device, but he would ride it all the way to town and back, a distance of ten miles, just to play the Pac Man video game at the local convenience store.

Larry Wise, longtime owner of Cosmopolitan Motors, was one of Ryan's early sponsors. Way back when Ryan was just a little kid, Larry expressed to me that he could tell Ryan possesses exceptional skills. Besides Larry, Ryan benefitted from sponsorship through unexpected sources, such as a family friend, Kenny Jones, as well as Ted Newmarker, a professional hockey player. Each of these folks evidently saw in Ryan, the potential for considerable achievement in observed trials.

Here's Ryan and my cousin, Chuck Roan, taken at the '87 World Round. Chuck contributed greatly to helping out at the '87 event, was particularly instrumental in coordinating with the Multiple Sclerosis group to provide volunteer assistance, and they in turn received a nice check for their services.

Another picture of Ryan at the '87 World Round. He was just 19 years old at the time, yet performed exceptionally well that day.

Irrespective of the investment of time and dedication required of Ryan to succeed in trials, he still managed to do very well academically, graduating from high school with honors. And as if riding his motorcycle wasn't enough, Ryan also excelled in observed trials bicycle competition. He did so well in fact that at one point, Jim Ellis provided Ryan with a trials bicycle specially built for him by Bill Grapevine. Ryan took the bike into competition and immediately went head-to-head with then-reigning US Bicycle Observed Trials Champion, Kevin Norton, taking second in that year's championship.

And keep in mind that we were just a poor, working-class family, so Ryan never had any of his bills paid for him despite his focus on competition. Nope, once out of school, he went right out and got himself a job, working for my friend, Bob Logue, at Bob's Honda motorcycle dealership. Together, all these things surely point to the basic nature of Ryan as well as all my kids. That is each and every one of them are go-getters. They never sat back and expected anything to be just given to them. Instead, they've each gone out and worked for everything they have and everything they have achieved. That alone makes me extremely proud as a father and I hope is a reflection of how the kids were raised.

This one was taken during the 1990 season, when Ryan and I were riding the Nationals. Can't quite remember exactly where we were in this photo, but both of us appear to have finished well—especially Ryan.

So, with high school out of the way, Ryan made the decision to work his way toward a national title in observed trials. He and I began traveling to and competing in as many national events as possible, and Ryan consistently improved his skills. He quickly adapted to traveling and to the variety of terrain and varied challenges at trials events all over the US. In short order, Ryan won the Sportsman National Championship then, in 1986, placed second in the pro class. Finally, in 1988, he put it all together and won his first National Professional Championship. What followed then was an amazing string of successes as Ryan did go on to win his six championships consecutively. And certainly, those titles did not come easy. Ryan faced tremendous competition and by great good fortune did not suffer any serious injuries throughout those six seasons. And in addition to his national championship titles, Ryan was selected to represent the United States numerous times in the International Trials Des Nations.

Further, it is worth noting that, in addition to his tremendous skill in the art of observed trials riding, Ryan is and has always been a very calculating competitor. Much of what he has accomplished is in part to Ryan's careful study of the sport itself and the rules which govern competition. Early on, Ryan became acutely aware of the mechanics of observed trials—how the bikes work and how they can used as efficiently and effectively as possible against any and all obstacles. Plus, Ryan spent considerable time studying the rule book in order to apply techniques in competition which could potentially provide him with any kind of advantage. It is our belief in fact that some of the newly applied techniques which Ryan employed led to implementation of updated rules for the sport.

Here again I can't remember the year or venue, but
Ryan is evidently serving as Minder for me.

Today, Ryan is happily married and works for Brad Baumert who, together with Ryan, created and developed Ryan Young Products, which is currently a company of international reach and scope. Additionally, Ryan hosts observed trials riding schools and still rides occasionally in competition. It was in fact in 2017, at the age of fifty, that Ryan achieved one of his most sought-after successes when he won Colorado's Ute Cup event. Ranked as one of the toughest observed trials events in the world, the Ute Cup challenges riders with exceptionally difficult terrain, high altitudes, and extreme conditions. A win at the Ute had eluded Ryan in numerous previous attempts, and for him to finally win it, and at fifty years of age, is truly a testament to my son's ability. I must point out also that the 2017 Ute was a real family affair for us as, in addition to Ryan, both Mike and I rode the event as well. By doing so, I became the oldest rider to ever compete in the Ute. Mike rode extremely well, and were it not for him hanging back to ride with me and serve as my minder, Mike would likely have finished very well in the event himself.

This was a very special event for each of us. Mike, after dedicating years to his family and his military career, was back into it and riding better than ever. In fact, were it not for Mike hanging back and riding with me, he may very well have earned a top finish in his class. As for myself, I couldn't be prouder of having become the oldest rider to ever compete in the Ute Cup. And Ryan—winning the prestigious Ute Cup at age 50, is nothing short of amazing. A tremendous demonstration of his skill and capabilities.

Another shot of Mike, Ryan, and I, taken at the 2017 Ute Cup. What an awesome event. I would rate it as one of my most favorite to ride.

In the end, I don't know how much my own skills may have contributed to Ryan's long-term success in the sport of trials. Did he inherit some innate abilities from me? Possibly. Did my guidance and training efforts benefit him? I like to think so. Did the time we spent together, traveling and competing, contribute to all those titles Ryan has won? I hope so. Regardless, I believe my relationship with Ryan, as well as with all my kids, has been, and continues to be, one of love, respect, and support. And if those efforts on my part have contributed to the positives in their lives, well, what more could a father ask for?

Ryan and I, and the Cub, were featured guests at a wonderful event held at the Broom Factory. During the course of the weekend we spent there, our hosts set up a series of studio photographs. This is one example.

CHAPTER 12

My Other Pursuits

What else have I done with my life?

I've described in a previous chapter my extensive involvement in the sport of archery, which began at an early age, both in competition and for hunting, so let's move on to what next captured my attention and interest.

Like most young guys growing up in the 1950s, I was really into cars. Customized cars, especially. Body modifications were a big thing back then, with a lot of chopping and channeling and other alterations to the way the car came from the factory. Everyone wanted to make their own car cool and distinctive—different from the rest.

A rather poor-quality picture, but it does provide a nice view of the Kaiser grill I was so proud to have adapted onto my car. This particular photo was taken rather early on in the whole process. There was much more work, and much refinement to follow.

By the time I was sixteen, I had already been working for a while and had saved up enough money to buy my own car—a 1950 Ford convertible. It was a nice car. Ran good, looked good. Ah, but I immediately began planning to customize it. There was this '51 Ford running around town that had been smoothed and altered and featured among other body modifications the front grill from a '55 Kaiser. That car really caught my attention as to me its grill looked like a shark's mouth, so I set my sights on setting my car up with that same type of front-end treatment. Well, wouldn't you know it but something happened to that guy's car, it broke down or he wrecked it or something, and I was able to buy the grill.

Installation of the grill certainly was not a bolt-on job. No, the entire font end of my Ford had to be modified and reshaped to accept it. Even at just sixteen years of age, I already had a good understanding of working with metal and handling a torch, so I tore right into the job. It was an extensive project too.

I cut and reshaped the hood, fabricated a separate brace to support the Kaiser grill, relocated the hood latch, and welded the hood to the front fenders, then cut new openings so that the hood opened entirely differently from the original layout. Next came the fill-in work. Although plastic "Bondo" products where available back then, as was common practice, I instead used lead to fill in imperfections and to shape and smooth contours. And as was the popular style at the time, I removed all the car's trim then leaded in all the holes left behind.

Keep in mind that this all took place over several years, with the car being continually worked on and reworked, as time and my modest finances permitted. Of course, we hot-rodded our cars too. Everyone wanted a fast car, and street racing was commonplace. You didn't want to be known around town as having a slow, uncompetitive car when it came to stoplight-to-stoplight drag racing. So, I did what I could to modify my car's flathead V-8. I rebuilt the engine and the transmission—the latter multiple times. All this was done by me personally too. There was no money to pay someone else to do the work, and we sure were not able to just order up speed parts online. No, it was simply a lot of elbow grease, and learning from your buddies, and applying what you learned and figured out along the way, as well as pulling a lot of parts out of the local junkyard.

In the end, I did have a good-looking, respectably fast car, several cars over time in fact, and greatly enjoyed the entire experience. Oh, and about those transmissions, they must have been a weak link in the Ford drivetrain as I kept breaking them. In fact, if memory serves, I went through twenty-three(!) three-speed manual transmissions and two automatics during the time I was hot-rodding around. Soon enough, however, my priorities changed as I met and married my first wife, started a family, and set about getting us all into a house. Money was as always tight, and with all I had learned from my father with respect to carpentry and plumbing and electrical work, I figured I could build my own house. We bought some property, had a foundation dug in, and I did actually pay a bricklayer to come in and lay up the block. However, although this guy started out the job at a pretty good pace, he soon became distracted with some other interests and let the job languish. Well, I had been watching him do the work, and helping all along the way, and figured I'd just finish the job myself. So, I mixed up the mortar, just like he did, applied it to the layers of block, set row of row, smoothed everything just as I'd seen it done, and before you knew it, the foundation was complete!

Next came the framework. A place right in town called Lundy Lumber had these do-it-yourself house plans. You looked over the plans, decided what kind of house you needed and could afford, and they prefabbed each wall then delivered them to the site. From there, it was just a matter of erecting the walls and securing everything in place. We next ordered the roof joists, got them in place, and had the entire house under roof in two days. Now, all the plumbing, electrical, drywall, and finish work took another eight months to complete, but with the help of my father and my wife and kids, we did it, and when all was said and done, we had ourselves a brand-new house. Still live there today, and I am pretty darn proud of us having basically constructed the entire place ourselves. Next up, sailing.

One day my second wife, Kelly, said to me, "We should be on the water." A very nice reservoir called Rose Valley Lake was right up the road from where we lived, and she had evidently been thinking about family activities in and around that facility. Thinking back on it now, Kelly may have originally thought we might end up with a motorboat of some kind. However, I went up to Rose Valley, saw all these sailboats out on the water, then went home and told her that we should get one. Kelly agreed to give it a try, so we bought ourselves a Pintail, built by a company called MFG. Now, here's the thing, neither Kelly or I knew a thing about sailing. But the way I figure it, there's nothing you couldn't learn. So, we bought a book that told us all about "how to sail" then went out and put it into practice. It took a while, of course, and we had our share of trial-and-error episodes, such as sinking the boat the very first time we launched it, but in the end, the whole family greatly enjoyed the experience of operating a sailboat.

The wife and the kids and I have since spent many wonderful hours on the water, sailing about in several different boats we've owned over the years. Of all our experiences, one in particular does stand out in my mind. It was our daughter Kaitlyn's fifteenth birthday, and she and I went up to Canandaigua Lake, in New York state. There's an old mansion on the lake which has been converted into a yacht club, and they were hosting catamaran races. Well, I was just a novice at the time, and it showed as we came in last place in each of the first three races of the weekend. It was a two-day event, and going into the fourth and final race, on Sunday, I was considering just loading up and leaving as another last-place finish appeared likely. However, an official approached me and explained that we were in line for the "Toilet Seat Award." Well, you can guess what that award was for, but hey, an award is an award, so we went back out, finished last, and indeed took home the coveted Toilet Seat—my first-ever sailing trophy. Kaitlyn and I had great fun regardless, and I promised myself on the way home that I would return the next year and do better.

With daughter, Kaitlyn, on her 16th birthday, competing in a regatta, on Lake Canandegwa, in New York state. We won the coveted toilet seat award that day.

Well, I did in fact go back the next year, this time with daughter Laura Lee. And with considerably improved skills by that time, more than made up for my poor showing the year before. Conditions for the event were quite challenging, with 30 mph winds and quite choppy water. Several boats capsized over the course of the weekend as a result. There were fifty-seven boats entered, and although I do not recall our exact finishing position, I do very well remember one particular shining moment. On one critical tum, we were to come about and begin moving with the wind. At first, I was prepared to move cautiously but changed my mind at the last moment and chose instead to go with a much riskier "jibe" maneuver. Basically, this means that the wind direction changes from one side of the boat to the other very quickly. Done improperly, this would surely have upset us, but this day luck and skill were on our side, and our little catamaran took off like a rocket, traveling at just the about the highest speed I ever experienced on a sailboat, passing thirteen other craft and crews in the process. It was exhilarating, and very satisfying, particularly when one of the other crews called out, "Very aggressive sailing, Jerry!"

I've also enjoyed some wonderful sailing experiences together with my longtime friend, Jim Ellis. Jim had been sailing for years and kept his boat at a family residence in Maine. Once Jim became aware that I had gotten into sailing, he invited me to join him. Jim would spend three weeks each year in Maine and eventually worked his way up from several smaller boats to a twenty-four-foot Marlin—a very nice, Harrishoff-design boat. I traveled to Maine many times to spend several weeks with Jim and accompany him in the Marlin into Casco Bay and out on the Atlantic Ocean. Quite an experience, very different from sailing on the flat water of Rose Valley Lake!

Never was much for power boats, but I sure enjoy sailing. There is a certain measure of satisfaction earned from learning how to operate a sailboat, and to conduct yourself well, out on the water.

This was taken during one of my trips up to Maine, to go sailing with Jim Ellis out on the Atlantic Ocean. Quite an experience!

As described earlier with respect to customizing my old cars, I am quite proud of my ability to work with metal. Continuing along those lines, I've since applied my talents to design, fabrication, and construction of various sculptures and awards. During the time I headed up the Pennsylvania Trials Riders, for example, I wanted the awards we handed out at our events to be unique and special—something much different from the standard store-bought-type of trophies. I started out by creating a branding iron featuring the PTR logo. I'd then cut up some nice pieces of wood, burn in the PTR logo, then finish up with a wood-burning tool to provide details specific to the individual awards. Other specialized, all-metal trophies followed as I worked to refine techniques specific to such work. It's all quite meticulous as most of these pieces are not just torch-cut and shaped hunks of metal. I typically highlight features and outline lettering of the basic metal with brass—a very tricky process indeed. The steel piece itself must first be heated red hot. I next dipped a brass rod into flux, heated the brass itself to just short of the melting point, then touched the brass to the red-hot steel. If all goes well, the brass flows just where I intend it to, and the process is repeated over and over until the final effect is achieved. Nothing was perfect, of course, and mistakes did inevitably occur. But you know what? In the end, it's art! And besides, I'm usually the only one aware of the mistakes.

The Pennsylvania Trials Riders organization—my lasting legacy.
I consider the formation, development, and continued existence
of this club, to be among my greatest accomplishments.

Among those pieces of my artwork, I am most proud of include one I made up to present to my parents on their fiftieth wedding anniversary. I also produced a large, elaborate award for Lane Levitt in honor of his 1974 Observed Trials National Championship. Not only was the award of considerable size and detail, but it also featured a candleholder on the back side. I placed the holder in just the right location so that once a candle was lit upon it, in a darkened room, the light produced casts a perfect outline of the sculpture on an adjacent wall. This award was designed and constructed without Lane's knowledge, with the intention of presenting it to him as a total surprise at the AMA awards banquet. Much to my disappointment, however, the AMA denied my plan. Once they saw a photograph of the award, the AMA indicated it was too distinctive, too different from all the other awards, and as such was deemed inappropriate. In the end though, Lane did receive the award, in private, and he has since told me repeatedly that after all these years, it remains his most favorite award.

My passion for working with metal, as with my interest in motorcycles, has stood the test of time. Each of these endeavors require considerable skill, and I like to think that I'm pretty good at both. I created this piece as a gift to my parents, in honor of their 50th wedding anniversary.

I worked a lot of details into this trophy, which celebrates Lane's 1974 championship. For example, in addition to Lane's likeness, look closely and you will see that the base is a map of the United States. And, highlighted on the map are the states in which Lane won National events that year. Plus, each of the stars represent a win. This is one of my most detailed works, and is among those I am most proud of.

My biggest, most complicated, difficult, and expensive piece to date is a commemorative, I guess I would call it a monument, dedicated to my club—the Pennsylvania Trials Riders. It measures 42 inches across by 48 inches tall, and once completed and set in place will sit atop a 30-inch-tall stone base—all constructed by me.

It will be on permanent display at the old Roaring Branch Motorsport facility, site of the 1978 World Championship round, which together with the PTR, I organized and hosted. Known today as Mill Hill Manor, it is currently owned and managed by a private sportsman club, which has generously agreed to provide the PTR monument with a permanent home. This piece has taken me years to plan and construct, and I consider it to be my most impressive to date. It is a way of providing something of long-lasting recognition to my creation and development of the Pennsylvania Trials Riders— my legacy. In addition, the monument celebrates all the workers and other fine people who contributed to making the '78 World Round a reality, as well as honoring Bernie Schreiber, America's first, and only, Observed Trials World Champion.

Three years of my life went into planning and construction of this monument. Quite frankly, a single photograph does not do it justice, as it is triangular, and three-sided. Two sides honor the PTR and my '78 World Round, while the third features a montage of photographs, with names of the riders who took part in the event. This photo was taken just prior to the monument being transported to its permanent home at the old Roaring Branch facility. It truly must be seen to be appreciated, as the details, all formed through work with torches on heavy metal, are quite intricate. I consider this my finest, although not final, work.

National and International Trials Events at Roaring Branch, Pennsylvania U.S.A

In September 1974 and November 1976 National Championship Observed Trials Rounds attracted scores of competitors and hundreds of spectators from all over the U.S. to this site. On June 11, 1978 another National Championship Round was paired with the Wagner Cup, the U.S. Round of the World Trials Championship.

Among the Europeans, five World or European Champions participated including Mick Andrews, Malcolm Rathmell and Martin Lampkin of Great Britain, Yrjo Vesterinen from Finland and Ulf Karlsson of Sweden. The many American riders were led by National Champions Lane Leavitt, Marland Whaley and Bernie Schreiber.

Held here at the Roaring Branch Motorsport Park, the 1978 event was so popular it caused a mile long traffic jam. After a Marine Corps Color Guard and the National Anthem, the crowd lined Cascade Run, a steep, ledge-filled mountain stream. Section after Section ran straight up numerous waterfalls. A twelve-foot-tall waterfall at the top of Cascade Run required carving a steep hillside trail out of the gorge for the riders and spectators.

At the end of the day a 19-year-old Californian, Bernie Schreiber on a Bultaco, won his third World Round after earlier wins in France and Spain. In 1979 he became the first, and as of 2018, the only American World Champion. From 1977 to 1987 Bernie was sponsored by Bultaco, Italjet, SWM and Yamaha, winning 20 of the 99 World Rounds he entered! Additionally, he was the 1982 Scottish Six Day Trial Winner and the U.S. National Champion four times.

The gate fees raised thousands of dollars for the Multiple Sclerosis Campaign. The Tech Inspection and the Introduction of Riders to the Press were held the previous day at the Genetti Lycoming Hotel in Williamsport. They also hosted the Awards Banquet where locally designed bronze plaques were presented.

These events were organized by the Pennsylvania Trials Riders Club with the very generous and dedicated help of hundreds of volunteers. All of this was only possible through the foresight and efforts of Rick and Dot VonGerbig who purchased this land and created the Park.

This Monument is a Tribute to all past, present and future Trials Riders. It is dedicated to everyone who helped in any way to make these National and International Trials Championship Events a reality. Finally, it is a Big Thank You to Mill Hill Manor for permitting this Historical Marker.

Latitude: 41.5751   Longitude: -76.9082

Here's the monument, in its final location, at Mill Hill Manor. Text above the images appears among the photographs on one of the three sides. It's difficult to really appreciate how the piece presents itself, from a two-dimensional photograph. Best to visit it in person! This entire area really is a beautiful part of the country, and well worth a stop if you are ever anywhere near Williamsport, PA. GPS coordinates are: Latitude 41.5751, Longitude 76.9082.

And with respect to all my years of working with metal, it all started with my father purchasing a set of torches for me for my sixteenth birthday. I could not have done any of this with that gift, and the instruction and guidance, which Dad in turn provided me.

Although observed trials riding has been my primary motor-cycling focus, I do certainly enjoy all aspects of the sport, and that includes riding on the street. I have owned various road bikes over the years, and like virtually everything in my life, I've never gone about it halfway. Case in point, some years back, I purchased a 1982 Honda CBXI000. Fabulous piece of equipment. Cross-the-frame six cylinder, smooth, quiet, fast. Plus, mine is one of the last of the CBXs, with the frame-mounted fairing and hard bags. And since such a machine definitely lent itself to long-distance travel, at one point, I decided to take my first cross-country ride. This was during the years when Bill Grapevine was hosting his great Past Masters Trials events each year out in Kansas, and I figured that riding out there and back would make for a great experience.

I contacted Bill, described what I intended to do, and asked if it were possible for him to provide me with a motorcycle to ride at the event. Bill assured me that he could make that happen, so I proceeded with my plans. Now, keep in mind that I was still working back then and did not have much time available to take off from work. Wasn't about to let that stop me though, so I set off right after work on Thursday and beelined it across six states, arriving just in time for the riders meeting on Saturday morning. I tried to get a little sleep before climbing onto the trials bike Bill had provided and head-ing out into competition, but I was just too keyed up. So, off I went and rode yet another fabulous Past Masters course. Late in day, after we'd finished up, I built a big bonfire in the camping area, which had become a tradition for me, and everyone pretty much figured I would soon pitch my tent and get some much-needed rest. "Nope," I said, "I've got to get back home for work on Monday morning."

And despite much protesting from my friends, I climbed back onto the CBX, and off I went. I would have made it, too, except that the CBX's headlight burned out during the night, early Monday morning, while I was crossing Ohio. Forced to stop, I pulled into a gas station, laid down in the grass over in a corner and waited for daylight. I did indeed get a bit of sleep, then got up and called my boss to tell him I would be late for work, and finished the trip, still managing to put in about a half day on the job. About 2,300 miles, including riding Saturday's Past Masters event, in about eighty-four hours, taking into consideration my forced stop on the way home, that was some run!

That experience whetted my appetite for more long-distance riding, and combining such a trip with participation in a trials event just made the whole experience that much better. So, I set my sights next on riding the CBX out to a National Observed Trials event in Southern California, and thanks to my son, Ryan, there was a motorcycle waiting for me there to compete on. Everything worked out great too. The bike once again performed flawlessly; I greatly enjoyed competing out there in California and wrapped up my trip by then traveling up the west coast and then heading back across the country to Pennsylvania.

So, how to top rides back and forth across the country? Why, a trip to Alaska, of course, so I made plans to do so. I wouldn't be alone this time, however. Through my friend, Bob Logue, I had been made aware that Bob's cousin, Chris, and his wife, Mary Beth, were planning a trip up to Alaska and were looking for someone to go along with them. I got together with those folks, and we compared notes on how we would like to go about the trip to assure that we'd all be compatible with one another. Satisfied that we could get along for a month, and many thousands of miles, we made our preparations.

My CBX had proven to be such a solid, totally reliable machine that I simply performed a tune up, installed new tires, a new chain, and sprockets—generously donated and installed by Bob Logue— changed the oil, and considered it ready to go. I had installed a taller windshield to supplement the Honda's factory fairing and also rigged myself up another little comfort feature. In preparation for many days of camping, I thought it would be beneficial to have available an option to sleeping on the ground every night. So, I actually rigged up a hammock of sorts, which would enable me to sleep up on top of the bike! That's right. With a little planning, and "Jerry-rigging," I had this setup to string a basic hammock from the front of the bike to the back. Little tricky climbing in and out of it, and in the end, I only used it a couple of times, but it worked. Lastly, I did take along two replacement rear tires—one for my CBX, and one for Chris's Honda Transalp.

Chris shipped his Transalp to Washington state so that he and Mary Beth could fly out there and reduce their total riding time. I, meanwhile, climbed aboard the CBX and headed out there to meet up with them. It was a yet another wonderful ride cross-country, and my only challenge came when I crossed the border into Canada. I must have appeared suspicious to the Canadians for some reason or another, and they made me unload and open up every piece of my luggage from the CBX, plus asked me a whole litany of questions. "Where was I going?" "Why?" "How long did I intend to stay?" "What resources did I have at my disposal?" I guess they didn't want some itinerant bum on a Honda CBX getting stranded in the Great White North with no way to get home. But they evidently decided that Jerry Young apparently posed no threat and sent me on my way.

There we are, at the Artic Circle. Still amazes me to think about having ridden a motorcycle that far. We were closer to Russia at this point, than we were to the continental U.S. How about that! Check out the two spare tires strapped onto my CBX. Both Chris and I each still own and ride these respective bikes.

Overall, the trip was really awesome. Chris and Mary Beth and I rode all the way north to the Arctic Circle, just to say we had done it.

There was a lot of great scenery but also much that was forgettable. A lot of low, scrubby vegetation the further north you go, and, of course, a lot of gravel roads. Not much in the way of any true riding challenges. I did, at one point, overcook it when arriving unexpectedly at an intersection. We were moving along pretty fast one day, trying to make it on time to get on board a scenic train ride. Crested a rise, and there just ahead was T-intersection. The road we were on connected there with the Alcan Highway, and while there was a road sign to warn of the upcoming intersection, I was half asleep at the time as the result of the extreme schedule I'd been maintaining. As a result, I was going *way* too fast and quickly worked to get the CBX slowed down while remaining in control. I got on the front brakes as hard as I could without locking up the front wheel while doing the same with the rear brake. The result was a series of three skid marks as I alternatingly locked and released the rear wheel. I slid right through the intersection—no traffic coming from either direction, thank goodness, and finally got stopped right against the berm on the other side. Amazing that I didn't crash or get hit by another vehicle running along the Alcan Highway! I got my nerves under control and was just about to get turned in the right direction when Chris came running up with his camera, hollering that he wanted to get a picture to document the event.

The balance of our ride was completed, fortunately, without any more such close calls, and after four weeks and some 12,700 miles covered, I was back home in Pennsylvania. Sharing stories of this experience with friends and family piqued the interest in particular of my son, Mike. Then after kicking around the idea for a while, he approached me about doing another Alaskan trip. It took a while to put everything together, but two years later, with having thirty days of leave available from his position with the military, Mike and I headed north. I was on the CBX once more while Mike had purchased a big Kawasaki four-cylinder road bike for the trip. Mike was living in Colorado at the time, and I rode out there and met up with him at his house. Once we had joined up, Mike and I made a pass through Glacier National Park then headed up the Trans-Alaska Highway. Accommodations once again mostly involved camping, and all went well such that by day thirteen, we had made it to Fairbanks. Mike indicated that he was satisfied we had made it that far, and given the time remaining to us, we turned for home.

We elected to take some different routes on our way back south, which led us to higher elevations where we experienced snow for the first time on our trip. At one point, there was about six inches of the white stuff on the ground, and the roads were considerably covered over. Riding eventually became quite dicey, so we elected to stop and wait for a snow plow to clear the road. Mike and I pulled off and waited, warming our hands on the bike engines, and in time, a plow did indeed come along. From there, road conditions, while still tricky, were manageable. Eventually, we worked our way down to lower elevations, and the snow turned to rain, and those were about the worst conditions we experienced throughout the trip. Interestingly, temperatures were for the most quite warm during our days on the road, and in fact on occasion, it became quite hot.

And so, I got another Alaskan trip under my belt. Other than a brief bit of rough running, which I suspected was the result of some poor quality fuel, the CBX functioned great, with no problems at all. Mike's Kawasaki similarly performed great. Not a hitch, and he was very pleased with the experience. In hindsight, I was very glad to have taken these trips. I got to see a lot of beautiful scenery, and all from the seat of a motorcycle. What could be better?

Over time I have managed to become capable of at least playing a
tune or two on my guitar. The au' naturelle pose? Just me having
a little fun, and exhibiting a bit of my free-spirited attitude.

Now, in an entirely different vein, back when I was in my twen-
ties, some guys I worked with invited me to go bowling with them at
the local Elks Club. Yep, the club has its own bowling alley down in
the basement. I wasn't a member but got in anyway. I'd hardly ever
bowled in my life, but I would get together with those guys once a
week or so, bowl a few games, share some laughs, and have a good
time. It was a nice way to break away from the typical routine of life,
especially during the winter months. I even won an award for my
efforts—a belt buckle, signifying "Most Improved Bowler." But family and other pursuits soon took precedent, and I moved on.

Years later, in my sixties, I decided to get back into it. Wintertime
in North Central Pennsylvania can be pretty dull, so here was a way
to once again meet up with friends and engage in a fun, competitive

activity. I joined a league and decided that, like everything else in my life, I was going to give it my very best effort. Plain and simple, I wanted to be better than the other guys, and to win! So, I asked questions about specific techniques and studied other bowlers, and sure enough, my scores began to improve. This then kicked in my desire to go ever further. I chose to take lessons. Got even better. I was truly learning things from the lessons and putting them into practice, effectively. And I was achieving better scores than virtually everyone I bowl against. I was winning! I've kept this up too.

I practice two to three times each week and have come very close several times to my ultimate goal of scoring a perfect game of 300. So, the whole thing with bowling, it's just like everything else I've done in my life. First, I want to be able to do it—simply participate in the sport or activity or whatever. Then I want to get better at it—continue to improve my own performance. Then comes competition. Those guys are good; I want to be better. And I want to win! It was a very strongly ingrained desire, which I've felt my entire life. That basic, competitive spirit, pushed me forward, driving me to work that much harder, focus more, practice more, study the whole process, and in end excel. It's been the basis of everything I've done in my life, and in all modesty, I am pretty darn good at a lot of things.

JERRY YOUNG RIDER PROFILE DATE OF BIRTH APRIL 13 1940

RODE THE 1991 SCOTTISH SIX DAY TRIAL FORT WILLIAM UK

PROMOTED NATIONALS 1974 76 78 81 86 91 94 96 01 05.

6 TIMES AMA NATC TRIALS CHAMPION SENIOR 35 1984

1972 1978 1979 AMA DISTRICT # 6 OBSERVED TRIALS CHAMPION

RODE THE 1970 BIRKSHIRE INTERNATIONAL 2 DAY TRIAL A 360 MILE EVENT.

MIDDLEFIELD MASSACHUSETTS RIDER # 353

1978 1987 WORLD CHAMPIONSHIP

CLERK OF COURSE

HOST ORGANIZER

ROARING BRANCH PA. AND BODINES PA.

RODE THE PASTMASTERS TRIAL FRADONIA KANSAS TEN YEARS IN A ROW.

FIRST PLACE CLASSIC 1994 FIRST OVERALL 1996.

1972 AMA EASTERN REGIONAL TRIALS NATIONAL CHAMPION

SENIOR 55 AMA NATC TRIALS CHAMPION 1996

MEMBER NATC 30 YEARS: INVENTED THE EXPERT SPORTSMAN CLASS AND

NATC HALL OF FAME.

SENIOR 45 AMA NATC TRIALS CHAMPION 1985 1986 1989 1990

1972 AMA NATIONAL OBSERVED TRIALS NATIONALCHAMPION

I was just doing a little cutting and pasting of photos one day, making up this little montage. Then I decided to list out some of my more noteworthy accomplishments. Before long, I started running out of room! Guess I really have accomplished a lot!

Chapter 13
Family and Friends

What Others Have to Say About Me

Throughout this book, I've been recollecting and telling stories all about myself—from my perspective, of course. Now here's the chance for you hear about Jerry Young from other people in their own words. So, here goes, and we'll see how well my reputation holds up.

First off is my wife, Kelly. Without her, I would certainly not be where I am today. Kelly has, each and every day, been wonderfully supportive and encouraging. Without her, much of what I have accomplished in my life simply would not have happened.

My lovely wife, enjoying life to the fullest.

Kelly Young

My introduction to the sport of observed trials was initiated through Jerry, of course. I loved going to the events with him and walking the loops. I also loved that Jerry spent so much time with his son, Ryan. Jerry and Ryan practiced riding together almost every day after work and school. They set up sections right out in our backyard, which were quite challenging.

Early on, when they were competing against one another, Jerry would always end up with a better score than Ryan. However, as he got older and his skills improved, Ryan kept getting closer and closer to matching his father's performance. Finally, the day came when Ryan outscored his father in trials. I felt sorry for Jerry. I remember asking Ryan, "Why would you beat your dad? That wasn't very nice." Obviously, I missed the point of trials competition entirely. I now laugh about that day.

When Jerry and I met, we were each already very involved with individual sports we are very passionate about. We made a strict pact with one another way back then, and that was that neither of us were permitted to say "no" with regard to one another's sport. And we never have. After all these years, Jerry and I continue to be fully supportive of one another. There is nothing more gratifying than participating in the sport you love. The camaraderie with fellow participants is so special! I feel sorry for anyone who has never experienced that. In fact, I feel that such connection and association with fellow enthusiasts in one's chosen sport is even more important than the sport itself. I am so thankful that trials has provided Jerry such wonderful camaraderie with his fellow competitors. Such feelings can never be duplicated or replaced.

I am also very thankful that trials has enabled Jerry to travel all over the United States and even to Scotland. As a result, he has been provided the opportunity to make so many great friends. Trials also provided the means for a father to spent a great deal of time with his children—two in particular. Mike and Ryan have a very special bond with their father and a love for the sport of trials, and what more could a parent ask for? Trials has also kept Jerry happy and contributed to keeping him healthy, and I am certainly thankful for that. With all this said, there is one side effect to observed trials that I find quite annoying—it puts some kind of spell on the participants, resulting in them obtaining and collecting all kinds of motorcycles. Trials bikes and road bikes and everything in between. That's the truth! I guess you can't ever have too many motorcycles though. At least that's what Jerry says.

Ryan Young

I could go on and on with stories about my father. There were so many experiences we have enjoyed and continue to enjoy together. Coming up with just one or two which stand out would be very difficult for me. Instead, I would like to reflect on all that Dad managed to achieve—simply to place us in a position to enjoy those experiences. So, I'll share a bit about what it took for us to get out and about, all over the country, and to ride and compete in trials events.

As has surely been mentioned elsewhere in the book, Dad is just an average, blue-collar guy, and so there were never a surplus of funds to provide elaborate means for us to travel, and for accommodations, as we chased the schedule of events around the country. There was never any big truck and trailer, and the luxury of hotels and restaurants were a rarity. Instead, Dad would make do with whatever vehicle he happened to have at the time, typically pulling an open trailer with the bikes on it. Tent camping was the general rule for overnight stays, and we almost always brought along our own food and cooked over a little camp stove.

Doing the Nationals with dad, in 1990. This is how it was. Living
out of the back of our tow vehicle. Note my bicycles on top
of the Suburban, as I was also competing in bicycle trials at
that time, and nearly won the championship that year.

Speaking of those tow vehicles, wow, Dad would find a way to make virtually anything work. The very first national event in which I competed was in Florida, and we made the trip in a Volkswagen Beetle. We were, of course, towing the bikes on an open trailer behind the bug, and packed into the little car were me, Dad, my stepmom, and a newborn, my stepsister Kaitlyn. With all four of us in the car, and towing the bikes, plus hauling camping gear as well as all our riding gear, gas cans, tools, and so forth, you can imagine how much the little car struggled. Regardless, Dad made it happen, drafting semis and shifting down into the lower gears to make the hills, hugging the edge of the slow lane, and hoping that no one would run us over.

And then there was the time we were making use of a little Honda Accord hatchback. It was just Dad and I this time, and I believe we were out in Utah. Anyway, we had camped out the night before the event and still had a way to go to get to where the event was being held. Well, wouldn't you know, we got a bit lost trying to find our way back onto the interstate from where we had camped and were running very late. Despite this, Dad just could not, or would not, drive fast to make up time, so I got behind the wheel, pushed the little Honda really hard, and managed to get lo the event in time to compete. Good thing, too, as that turned out to be my very first national win. And, of course, we traveled through all kinds of severe weather. On one trip in that crazy homemade Suburban camper of Dad's, we were driving through a terrible snowstorm in Colorado. All the big tractor-trailer rigs were traveling quite slowly in the right lane, too slow for Dad evidently as despite the road conditions, he steered us into the left lane in an attempt to pass the trucks. We all hung on for dear life inside the camper as our overloaded truck slipped and weaved through the deep snow. But, as always, Dad pulled it off, and we came through unscathed.

And the camping. Oh, boy, did we have plenty of interesting experiences while camping. All kinds of weather—hot, cold, wet, you name it. I remember in particular the first year that Dad and I elected to pursue the national championship for me. We had carefully planned our entire itinerary—all the dates, the locations, the traveling, the logistics, and what our estimated expenses were going to be for it all. Well, Dad, of course, had it figured to where we would make the trip, compete, and return, arriving back home having just expended the very last of our funds. No credit cards to fall back on, it was all cash then. I have so many memories of sleeping in tents and eating soggy cereal, arriving at the events feeling cold, tired, and a bit ragged while my competitors typically showed up fresh from an overnight stay in a comfortable hotel bed and had just eaten a big, hot breakfast. But I'll tell you, being in that circumstance made me want to succeed all that much more. Experiencing a bit of hardship cemented my desire to overcome the odds and to win. So, in the end, I have no regrets over the fact that Dad and I had to "rough it" a bit in order to get me out there to compete and eventually earn my national championships.

In summary, I have learned so much from my father, with respect to so many things. He has truly taught me perseverance and to apply myself logically to every and any challenge which comes my way. Take for example, the fact the we live in North Central Pennsylvania, where the winters are quite severe. Succeeding at the highest levels in any endeavor does not permit "taking time off," no matter what the circumstances. So, how does a trials rider train year-round when the ground is covered with ice and snow a good four or five months out of the year? Well, Dad and I had a really challenging little rocky section picked out along the loop he had laid out on our property. We would go out there in the winter and spread hot ashes from our wood burner along the preferred line through the section, and I would practice. I am so grateful for that experience, too, because working through such circumstances taught me more about traction control and body positioning than I could have learned any other way.

Also, Dad taught me so much practical understanding with regard to simply figuring things out. There were times when we had to make roadside repairs to our vehicles while out on the road, for example. I would ask him "How did you know what was wrong with the car?" as he performed the repairs. Dad would explain what evidence he derived from the circumstances and what steps he took in using the information gathered to come up with a diagnosis and eventually make the necessary repairs. From these and many other examples, I learned from his basic sense of logic and understanding and have applied it to everything I do in my life.

There is so much more I could talk about in regard to my father, but I am going to simply say that he has taught me everything I know and is the best Dad in the world.

Mike Young

When it comes to my father's riding ability, and in particular his skills aboard a trials bike, there is one memory in particular which really stands out. Included in the book is a picture of me aboard a little mini-trials bike. The machine is based on a 1974 Chaparral 80 and was made for me by Bill Grapevine.

That's me, at about ten years of age. I'm aboard the little Chaparral, which Bill Grapevine built into a trials bike for me. You can certainly tell why we nicknamed it "The Pumpkin".

Fondly referred to by us as "the Pumpkin" due to the orange color of its fuel tank, the little bike is, of course, not a full-on trials bike but worked reasonably well at the time for a youngster of my size and weight. So, one time, we were riding out at Tom Clemens's place, and it was cold enough that there was crusty ice in the creek, and the ground was muddy and slippery—definitely quite challenging for riding. It was so challenging in fact that no one was willing to, or able to, ride up the creek section we had laid out. And yet just to show that it could be done, my dad rode the Pumpkin up that section and cleaned it! That was tremendously impressive. All the other guys, with their full-sized, dedicated trials bikes just looked on in amazement. And this is just one example of what a terrific role model my father has been.

Dad's activities provided many terrific experiences for me as a kid growing up. I very well remember helping him work on his Cub and how I would look forward to going to the trials events. The nationals were particularly exciting as Dad would arrange for me to take time off from school so we could travel to the events and participate. Well before I began riding in competition, I would run along after the riders from section to section and greatly enjoyed the thrill of holding national and international-level rider's bikes for them as they walked sections. I guess few, if any of the bikes, featured kickstands back then, so I basically filled in as a mobile kickstand. Now imagine that, a kid my age rubbing elbows with the best riders in the world and getting to handle their machines. It was quite the thrill, and I loved it. My parents quite often had these top riders stay over at our house when they were in the area, and, of course, I got to meet them all! It was very exciting for a young man so interested in motorcycling.

Dad's successes as a rider speak for themselves, but as much as anyone in the US, he also contributed tremendously to promoting the sport of observed trials. I think most people would agree that, along with a few other key individuals, my father has been one of the driving forces behind observed trials in this country and very much helped to make the sport what it is today. Even back in the early days, Dad would work so hard at promoting his and other trials events. Everyone in the family would pitch in to help my father send out personal invitations, encouraging riders to come out and ride the events. My sister would fill out names and addresses on the envelopes, and Ryan and I would lick dozens of stamps and apply them. Dad never stopped working at making trials better and better.

There is no doubt in my mind that a big part of Dad's achievements, and his general popularity, is the result of his wonderful personality. He is simply a very likable guy and goes out of his way to reach out to everyone and anyone he comes in contact with. This was so very evident when traveling with Dad back when I was younger. Everywhere we went, everyone knew him. It was like having a celebrity for a father. Everyone just loves the guy! Even as an adult, when I would accompany Dad to events, such as the NATC meetings out in Colorado, I would be amazed at how well he was received by everyone at the very top of the sport.

One of our more recent experiences, and one of any favorite times with Dad, was when he and I and Ryan rode the 2017 Ute Cup together. Dad expressed regret that he rode but one loop (Saturday), but that in itself was a tremendous accomplishment for a man of his age, and we all greatly enjoyed ourselves. It was an awesome time and truly cemented just how great the sport of trials has been for our family.

Looking back, I have to say that Dad provided a wonderful life for me. Introduction to the sport that I still enjoy today, all the great experiences that came as a result of being a part of his activities and participation, and simply being the son of such a terrific and popular guy just overwhelms me. My father is a great guy and has done so much for the sport of motorcycling in general, and observed trials in particular; he should be in the Hall of Fame. And that's something we need to work on.

We don't get together nearly as often as we would like to these days. Fortunately, dad and Ryan and I have made it a point to now and then connect up at certain events.

Laura Lee Young-Bollman

I like to think that much of who I am today is largely the result of my father's influence. He instilled in me, as well as in my brothers and sisters, a love for life and an appreciation of all that we have been blessed with. I can, for example, trace my own skills involving art and music to standards that my father set for all of us kids while we were growing up. He also led me to appreciate, and enjoy to this day, the out of doors, nature walks, sailing, and certainly the appreciation of good food. I also feel that I inherited his social gene—his ability to communicate and work well with other people.

Dad is certainly a most intriguing individual. Once he gets something in his head, he sets a plan and perseveres until he has accomplished what he has set out to do. And he always has set lofty goals too. Dad has always carried a great love and passion for any activity he has ever become involved with. Plus, he is exceptionally detail-oriented.

I have many fond memories from growing up. Dad exposed all us kids to so many interesting experiences. He was always anxious to share his own activities with each of us. I remember, for example, helping him out in the shop while he was working on his motorcycle or any one of a number of other projects. Dad would always take the time to explain to me what it was that he was doing, how things worked, and each step in how he accomplished various tasks. Dad would also take me along at times while he was out working in the field, visiting various regulator stations. It was during these excursions that I learned to drive a car too. Well before I was old enough to have a license, Dad would get me behind the wheel out on hack country roads, and off we would go—Dad sitting in the passenger seat and encouraging me while I steered and did my best to reach the pedals. Dad once described to me how many of his working hours were spent in solitude, and it was this "quiet time" which enabled him to think, plan, and prepare for many of the things he has accomplished in his life.

And then, of course, there were all the wonderful experiences at trials events. It was very exciting, visiting different places and being around all the riders. And those experiences taught me a lot, too, as it was while we were a part of the trials scene that I came to understand Dad's competitive spirit and to appreciate his drive to succeed. And Dad certainly taught all us kids the value of a dollar. Dad never spoke much about money while my brothers and sisters and I were growing up. We just came to understand how to pinch pennies and to make do with what we had. In the end, Dad always figured out a way to take care of all of us and make things happen, with what resources we had available.

I'm sure everyone would agree that, as much as any other trait my father possesses, it has always been his social skills and personality which have helped him to excel in all his life's endeavors. It's almost like Dad has a certain aura about him. He literally attracts people and is so good at socializing and associating with virtually everyone and anyone he has ever come in contact with. And how does he do it? Well, it just seems that Dad is not only exceptionally friendly and communicative, but he is also at all times open and honest, always says just what is on his mind yet in a very nice way. My feelings are that God puts good thoughts into us, and my dad is exceptionally gifted at expressing those thoughts with very positive words and actions.

A recent picture of dad and I, taken one day when we were just out doing a little shopping in downtown Williamsport. I like to think that dad bestowed in each of us kids, clear minds, a strong work ethic, and the feeling that we could accomplish anything we chose to pursue.

Bernie Schreiber

To my best recollection, I first met Jerry alone of the Ute Cup events back in the early '70s. I knew Jerry was a serious competitor at the national level and recall his very smooth style. It was, however, at the 1978 world round, which Jerry hosted, when I really came to appreciate and respect his efforts on behalf of the sport. Jerry's event was what every international trials competition should be. It was held at a beautiful facility, the sections featured truly challenging obstacles, with multiple line options, and was in every way very professionally conducted. Additionally, Jerry's event was particularly memorable for me as it was my first-ever US victory in international competition. Riding his world round in the Pennsylvania mountains led me to understand and appreciate that smooth style of Jerry's—a style which is necessary, considering all the mud, water, and slippery rocks he consistently rides and trains on.

I've spent a good deal of time with Jerry since then and even stayed at his house. He has a wonderful family, and during my time at his place, the Young house was filled with love and fun and was full of motorcycles as well. I have known Jerry to be a true gentleman, always willing to help out a fellow rider—including me! On several occasions, at various events, I have approached Jerry for assistance while out on loops, and he never failed to come through, with parts or whatever I needed. He has been a tremendous supporter of observed trials and, along with his son, Ryan, has truly impacted the sport. Thank you, Jerry, for all you have done.

Wiltz Wagner

When I first got started in observed trials riding, back in the 1960's, the sport was not popular at all. There were few events, only a small number of participants, and no purpose-built observed trials motorcycles. People would show up on all kinds of bikes. I even remember seeing flat-track bikes at trials events with low pipes! And I certainly was among those trying to make do with a motorcycle, which applied poorly to trials. Spent a lot of time crashing, too, as I recall.

Promotion was fragmented back then, and no one was traveling long-distant events. Coordinating the efforts of far-flung promoters seemed to be a logical step toward moving the whole thing forward, so along about the early '70s, we initiated the North American Trials Council. Note, we included "North American" in the title right from the start as the intention always was to include the folks up in Canada.

Invitations went out to every trials group we could identify, and, quite fortunately, everyone showed up. We had representatives from multiple regional organizations, one of which was Jerry Young. And it all worked out. We discussed our knowledge of how to do all that is necessary to put on successful events, mixed and matched formulas, and in the end hatched out a plan which worked well enough to make the whole thing happen, the basis of which continues to this day.

Having known Jerry Young all these years now, I can look back and say with confidence that "the whole thing" worked as the result of "a Jerry mentality," which is simply the attitude of refusal of permitting things to not happen. And that's another way of describing a basic can-do attitude. Jerry wasn't the only individual in our group to possess this outlook, but he certainly epitomizes such. Few are the individuals I have come to know in my life who possess the sheer will and determination of Jerry Young. Once he gets an idea in his head, you can be certain that Jerry will see it through. Plus, few are the people who, like Jerry, never went away. That is Jerry has stayed with the sport, riding, promoting, and supporting at the highest level for decades.

One cannot overestimate the importance of Jerry's contributions to the sport of observed trials. There have been many, of course, but one which stands out in my mind is the 1978 World Round. With this event, Jerry brought to the United States the very best of what international observed trials competition can be. That event featured the most impressive riding and spectating experience one could ask for. It was indeed a most professional, enjoyable, and successful event.

In summary, my longtime friend, Jerry Young, what a character. A virtual wild man. He is a terrific guy. Very funny, very smart—a unique kind of smart too. In short, Jerry possesses a rare combination of intellect and practicality, great intelligence, plus true hands-on capabilities. He can envision things and then create them. Plus, he is flexible enough to rebound from things that don't work and see his way through to an alternative, which does work. Jerry and his son, Ryan, both have been an integral part of the development of the sport of observed trials. We owe much to them both.

Indeed, there I am at Jerry's '78 World Round. This photo indicates clearly just how tough the sections were. To his credit, Jerry rode all them first, proving by way of his own skills that each and every obstacle was manageable.

Jim Ellis

Jerry and I have known each other for many years, and he is certainly a very dear friend. As is chronicled elsewhere in this book, Jerry and I were considerably involved in assisting Bill Grapevine in his efforts to produce and market Bill's GRM motorcycles. And, has been described previously, I first met Jerry in 1972 at a Candytown

160

observed trials event. I showed up there with one of Bill's early GRMs, and Jerry came over to check it out. I offered to let Jerry ride the bike, which he did. Now, I'll be the first to admit that the GRM was not the best observed trials bike out there, but despite that, and the fact that Jerry had never even seen the bike before, let alone ridden one, he promptly and quite effortlessly took the GRM up and over a rock, which was about the size of a Volkswagen Beetle. Duly impressed, I began discussions with Jerry in regard to Bill Grapevine's ambitions, and the rest is history.

Although Jerry and I have enjoyed many, many motorcycling experiences over the years, including having ridden every one of Bill Grapevine's Past Masters events, I believe some of my best memories with him involve the times together out on the water sailing. I have access to a family home near Portland, Maine, on Casco Bay, and spend several weeks a year up there. Having become aware that Jerry was doing some sailing at home in Pennsylvania on a little puddle of a lake, I invited him to join me in Maine to try his hand at running some "real" water. Jerry took me up on the offer and brought along his 17-foot boat. We started out in Jerry's boat, sailing down the Royal River toward the bay. Well, Jerry promptly ran us aground as he didn't know anything about charts or channel markers, but we got pulled back into deeper waters and continued on. Once into the hay, Jerry pointed out what he thought to the oddly colored rocks on one of the nearby islands, except the rocks were moving! Jerry had never before seen harbor seals!

We sailed Jerry's boat to my family's cottage, which is located on Prince's Point in Yarmouth, Maine. There, we worked on my boat then took it out on an overnight trip, during which we encountered fog so thick that we had to rely entirely on the compass and charts to find our way—no GPS or satellite navigation available at that time! On the way back the next day, the wind died down until we were completely becalmed. I decided to take a nap to wait out the wind while Jerry stayed up on deck. When I rejoined Jerry after my little siesta, he excitedly described how he had witnessed a lobster trap buoy, not once but twice, disappear beneath the surface, only to reappear shortly after, evidently the result of those harbor seals tugging at the lines. I asked Jerry why he had not alerted me to what he perceived as a very unusual situation. He said that he just could not believe what he was seeing.

Overall, these and many other experiences with Jerry, both on the motorcycles and on our sailing adventures, were made all that much more enjoyable due to Jerry's unfailingly positive outlook and pure excitement involving our activities. He is certainly a man who enjoys life and the pursuit of fun and adventure. My own life has been greatly enriched as the result of my relationship with Jerry Young.

Bob Wentzel

I have come to know Jerry Young as not only a champion motorcycle competitor and a tremendously influential individual in the world of observed trials but also as a very close friend. This is my personal tribute to an amazing man.

The Trials Guru

I met this man a few years ago.
Thought he was someone I would like to know.
Trials riding is his love.
For his age, he goes beyond and above.
His history is long and exciting.
Years of knowledge and know-how is what he brings.
Crisscrossing the country with his sons,
The talent in that family, in their blood it runs.
A 1972 AMA National Championship.
Years later, a beat he does not skip.
You can see him at world rounds, nationals, and at local events,
His presence is noticed that what he represents.
A tough competitor to this day,
Glad to know this man is what I say.
You may see him on a Sherco or on a Triumph Cub,
Or maybe telling stories in a local pub.
Either way, his contribution to trials is amazing,
There was always a trail he was blazing.

He likes to sleep in his van.
Sometimes he eats out of a can.
I've seen him strum his guitar.
He's one of the best trials riders by far.
One thing for sure, I'd like to tell you,
This man, Jerry Young, is a trials *guru*!

Jerry and I, together with the great John Penton. Picture was
taken at a York Swap Meet event. Although he is sitting down in
this image, Jerry and I had to hustle to get the shot, because even
at age 94(!) Mr. Penton was still continually on the move.

Ed Fisher

I first met Jerry back in the '60s at a Candytown observed trials event. I wasn't a trials rider, but back then, I was game for any motorcycle event which I had the opportunity to ride. Like Jerry, I was riding a basic, original Triumph Cub. I do not possess Jerry's skills, however, and I was having quite a difficult time of it out in some of the more challenging sections. One of the sections in particular had me stopped dead as I couldn't make it up a hill. Wouldn't you know it, but of all the people there, spectating and competing, Jerry was the one person who stopped to help me, which is just the kind of guy he is. And we've been friends ever since.

One of my favorite experiences with Jerry occurred some years after. My wife and I were at the Laconia road races, and Jerry had ridden in on his Honda CBX street bike to spectate at the event. There was an Observed Trials competition taking place that weekend in addition to the other scheduled events, and once the organizers found out that Jerry Young was present, they asked him to participate. Jerry did not have his trials bike with him, of course, but he was told a bike would be provided for him. Jerry expressed his appreciation but indicated that his road-riding gear was not practical to wear for trials riding. The organizers said they would get him anything he needed. So, Jerry did ride the event on a borrowed, unfamiliar bike, wearing someone else's gear and won! And that right there tells you just how good of a motorcycle rider Jerry Young is.

Dave Henry

Jerry has described how, when he first began trail riding his Cub, he hooked up with some enduro riders. Well, I was one of those riders! I was competing on a Bultaco Matador back then, and although I didn't know Jerry at the time, we grew up in the same town, and it was inevitable that since we were both into off-road riding, we were going to run into each other at some point. So, a few of us got together one weekend at my brother-in-law Tim Scott's place. Tim owns quite a bit of property, and we were just going to do some trail riding. One of the guys, who showed up was Jerry, and he was, of course, riding his Triumph Cub. This was back when Jerry had first begun riding off-road, and, not knowing his skill level, we just took off and rode the trails at a pace we were used to. I'll give Jerry a lot of credit because he followed us wherever we went and tried his best to keep up. However, each and every time I looked back to check on Jerry, he was on the ground. And quite honestly, that is my favorite memory of Jerry Young.

Jerry, of course, went on to develop tremendous skills in motorcycling riding and competition, but you know, everyone must start out somewhere. So, with great respect to one of the best motorcycle riders I've ever known, I'll always remember seeing Jerry on the ground, time after time that day.

As a follow-up, Jerry and I have become great friends since that day we first met. As he progressed in the sport of observed trials, and eventually graduated from his Triumph Cub to an Ossa MAR, Jerry encouraged many of us to become more involved in trials as well. In fact, soon after Jerry began riding his MAR, I got one as well. And such became my level of interest and participation in trials that Jerry signed me up as one of the founding members of the Pennsylvania Trials Riders.

All these years later, I am overwhelmed by how much Jerry has accomplished in observed trials and other aspects of motorcycling as well as in his life in general. I am very proud to say that I knew him back when he first started out.

Tom Maneval

I've known Jerry Young since we were both little kids, having also grown up in Jerry's hometown of Williamsport, Pennsylvania. Early on, I knew Jerry as "one of them boys from up the crick road." I've got some deep roots in our area in North Central Pennsylvania as, among other things, my father and I surveyed the property which would eventually become the Roaring Branch facility, where Jerry's first international event was held.

Like Jerry, I'm an old trials rider from way back: rode a 247 Cota back in the early days, have been involved with PTR since it started, and helped put on the first international event, among many others. Those were great times, and it was awesome to have world-class riders come to Pennsylvania to ride events we ourselves put on. It was amazing to see the level of skill that top riders possess. For example, out working the sections on that first international, I soon assigned a nickname to Bernie Schreiber. I called him "Crash Bang" because even from a distance, you could hear Bernie slamming his Bultaco up against the rocks while negotiating sections. Tremendously impressive and aggressive!

So, a couple of stories about Jerry. One time, we were out trail riding and pulled up in front of this big wall of rocks. None of us have ever attempted to climb up there, and I didn't think anyone would even try. And yet after studying the challenge for a minute or two, Jerry said that he thought he could get up there. Much to our amazement, Jerry did indeed make it to the top—and on his first try!

There was nowhere to go once he got up there, however, except to come right straight back down. There wasn't even space to turn the bike around, but Jerry got off, lifted and turned his bike, and proceeded back down—and fast! There was no slowing the bike at all as it was virtually a free fall. That was one of the most impressive things that I've seen Jerry, or anyone, do on a motorcycle.

I also have to say that I've always been impressed by Jerry's tremendous optimism and good luck. He's the kind of guy who would load up his van, with four bald tires, travel a considerable distance to a trials event, and make it back home, without experiencing a blowout or a flat tire. And then there were Jerry's famous "directions." He would tell us how to get somewhere, with instructions which included something like, "Go down such and such a road for so many miles then turn down the lane next to the barn." Well, we would get out there, and there would be barns everywhere, and every one of them would have a lane next to it! To sum up my recollections of Jerry, he has always been up for a ride and always up for a party. And that's Jerry Young.

Tom Clemens

I'm from the same town as Jerry and in fact grew up in the same neighborhood as he did, so we've known each other since we were kids. We were buddies since way back then and had many fun times together while growing up. A few of our experiences really stand out in my mind, such as when Jerry and I were in high school and were out driving around in his Ford convertible. Jerry was doing a little showing off, speed shifting and really letting the Ford's loud pipes roar. But then someone turned in front of us, and Jerry couldn't quite get stopped in time. No seat belts back then, of course, and I flew forward and actually busted out the windshield with my head! But we were just seventeen years old, and I simply shook it off.

I got into motorcycling just about the time Jerry did, and we certainly had our share of adventures and misadventures. Take the time we were out riding and stopped at a restaurant to grab a burger or a coke or something. Well, out in the parking lot, Jerry started popping wheelies on his little Triumph Cub, and away he went across the parking lot, just impressing the heck out of himself and everyone else. He was doing a pretty good job of it, too, until the Cub's front wheel fell off! I can't remember the exact circumstances, but whatever mechanical issue led to the wheel dropping off, it obviously occurred right in the middle of one of Jerry's wheelies. He kept his cool though and got the bike slowed down to just a walking pace before allowing the front end to drop. Jerry jumped off and rolled on the ground a bit, much to everyone's amusement, of course. He was unhurt, fortunately, and the Cub was undamaged, so we simply remounted the wheel, and off we went again.

Much of our local trail-riding experiences came about on my property. I had about sixty acres and had all kinds of trails laid out. I was riding a Hodaka back then, and we would hit the trails pretty much year-round. I even went so far as to drill out the Hodaka's knobbies and build my own studded tires in order to deal with snow and ice. We didn't let anything stop us back then. I was one of the early members of the Pennsylvania Trials Riders and enjoyed many, many wonderful experiences as part of that group—both riding in events as well as assisting Jerry in putting on trials competitions. As Jerry advanced in pursuit of various trials events around the country, it would sometimes be months or even a year between times I would see him. Between work and riding, he was simply that busy. Such was Jerry's dedication to the sport and to his ambitions.

Several things come to mind when I think about the kind of guy Jerry is. For one thing, he is most certainly an exceptionally skilled motorcycle rider. As much as anything else, I have always been amazed at his ability to place the motorcycle exactly where he wanted it to be in the environment of observed trials riding. His body-placement ability, I believe, is one of the factors which really helped him to succeed. If you watch Jerry carefully, and if you know what you're looking at, you can tell that he is always perfectly positioned on the motorcycle. But, of course, that's just one factor which contributed to his great success in the sport. Another of Jerry's attributes which really impresses me is that he is quite simply really "sharp." What I mean by that is Jerry is very good at applying himself to anything he wants to accomplish, no matter what the job or the obstacle or the challenge. Jerry always finds a way to "get it done."

Look at what he did with that old Triumph Cub. Jerry did so much work on that little bike, it's just amazing. Just the frame alterations he performed and all with a gas torch. That work really should have been done with an arc welder, but Jerry made it work in his own way. Plus, Jerry is so methodical. He figures things out, never gets mad, and gets it done. Jerry is, and always has been, simply a good, honest Joe too. He is a great guy whom everyone likes. And those are my thoughts on Jerry Young.

Bob Logue

I first met Jerry when I opened my Honda shop back in 1978. He was already a local legend at the time, having firmly established himself as a key player in motorcycling, especially with respect to observed trials, of course. Jerry actually worked part-time for me for a while, helping out in the shop with sales and other efforts. He also greatly contributed in assisting me with putting on a trials event on the property of my own farm and, then several years later, actually hosting a national at my place.

So, what kind of a guy is Jerry? Well, he is for certain a take-charge kind of guy. The man knows what it takes to get things done and how to do it. There always have been multiple "spark plugs" driving the success of the Pennsylvania Trials Riders, for example, but as the founder, Jerry always was the Grand Pooba. He's the one who made things happen, period.

Jerry is, of course, a master of observed trials riding. I've never met anyone with more determination to master the art of our unique sport, and that certainly has contributed greatly to Jerry's riding achievements. Going anywhere and doing anything with Jerry is great fun as he knows people everywhere. Jerry is treated like a celebrity wherever he goes too. And Jerry's achievements go way beyond what he has accomplished involving his riding. The man is exceptionally intelligent and possesses a practical sense, which he definitely applies to mechanical work, fabrication, his skills in working with metal, and much, much more.

I could tell plenty of stories about how Jerry has applied his practical and conservative sense to various challenges. Take for example the time he was coming back from some event out of state, and the generator failed in his old Suburban. Did Jerry let this slow him down or force immediate repairs? Nope. Jerry instead strapped onto the roof of the Suburban, the Honda generator he had along for use in camp, fired it up, and drove down the road with that generator, providing juice to keep him on the road.

In short, I am very proud to call Jerry a friend.

Jerry is a truly amazing guy. A man of many, many talents, and great accomplishments. We've had a lot of fun together over the years.

Dave Bowen

Jerry Young is most certainly a very interesting person. I first met him back in my early days of dirt bike riding, and it was Jerry who introduced me to observed trials. Things were pretty basic back then. There were few dedicated trials bikes around, and most of us were riding modified trail bikes, such as the little Hodaka that I was competing on. Jerry and I rode a lot together, and I eventually bought two GRM motorcycle from him—one which I still own.

Those were great times back then, and I was very fortunate to be a part of all that Jerry had going on. Of course, we were young and passionate about the sport, and with Jerry leading the way, it seemed as if there was nothing we could not accomplish. So many fond memories working on setting up trials sections, riding various events, traveling around. One of my favorite riding experiences was when I accompanied Jerry over to Rhode Island, where I rode my first national trials event.

I cannot say enough about how important Jerry has been to the sport of trials—the things he accomplished both as a rider and as an organizer. I mean, he brought the world to Roaring Branch in Pennsylvania! How can you top that? Many, many people owe tremendously to Jerry Young, and that certainly includes me. His influence was, and is, truly amazing. He was a beacon in my life and opened up a whole world of people, places, and experiences for me. Jerry, I thank you, and the entire motorcycling community thanks you.

Adam Blumborst

I first met Jerry Young in 1995 at a national trials event in Hershey, Pennsylvania. I was just a nobody kid at the time, and the event was my first-ever national. Jerry was working tech inspection, and while going over my bike, we discovered an issue which was going to prevent me from riding. One of the bike's foot peg mounts was cracked and required welding. Despite his many other obligations that day, and not knowing me, Adam, Jerry took the time to locate a local weld shop, which resulted in completion of the necessary repairs, and assured that I was indeed able to ride my first national. I've never forgotten that act of kindness and consideration.

Since then, I have continued my involvement in the sport of observed trials and, as of the writing of this book, am current president of Trials Incorporated, plus have been serving as a minder for pros out on the national circuit. All along the path of my progression to where I am now, Jerry has always been there. I only wish I could have seen him competing when he was in his prime. I still remember talking with Jerry at a national in 1997, at which time I had just moved up to the expert class. Jerry congratulated me and expressed that it was unfortunate he and I would not be competing head-to-head as he had elected to step down from expert to advanced. I felt a bit sad for Jerry, yet he in turn was very happy for me to have made expert.

Despite my participation in the sport coming toward the end of his more serious competition involvement, I nonetheless learned a great deal from studying Jerry's techniques. From watching him carefully, I found that Jerry plans out every move in every section in advance. He then rides the exact line he walked, in every section, every time. As a rider, Jerry is exceptionally smooth. There is never any wasted energy in his riding style. Every move he makes is to accomplish exactly what needs to be done, nothing more, nothing less.

As a man, Jerry Young is the "open arms of the sport of observed trials." Whenever you see him, Jerry is genuinely happy to see you. No matter how busy he may be, Jerry always takes the time to talk with you and to inquire about how you are doing. He is largely responsible for bringing a great many people into the sport of observed trials—and keeping them involved!

Now, no story about Jerry Young is complete without discussion of his famous Triumph Tiger Cub. That bike, it looks like some crazy science experiment gone bad. The thing is I have the great fortune to have ridden the little Cub, on several occasions, and this is where the really crazy part comes in—the bike works! Incredibly well! That bike goes and turns and stops and does everything you need it to do amazingly well. Just don't look down while you're riding and see what a crazy-looking contraption it is. That little Triumph, all in itself, tells the entire story of Jerry Young—his ingenuity, extensive skill set, perseverance, and absolute will to make things happen—all contained in the most unlikely little machine you can imagine.

I have many, many wonderful stories from my own personal experiences with Jerry, but one memory in particular comes to mind to provide some insight into what he is all about. We were at a national in 2015, and Jerry showed up with that crazy little Cub. I went over to checked on him, and as always, Jerry expressed sincere happiness to see me. He invited me to visit with him for a while, and we sat down to talk. Jerry then opened up his cooler and offered to share with me what he had inside—a bottle of whisky, plus some tomatoes and celery, both of which were grown in Jerry's own garden. At that moment, looking at this kind and gentle man, who was nonetheless such a fierce and successful competitor, sitting there in his modest camp, with his funky old truck and even funkier old Cub, it's just hard to express how I feel about him. He is so down-to-earth. You just will never meet a better person than this man. Jerry Young is a "face-value" guy. He always speaks the truth, be it good or bad, yet never fails to make you feel good about yourself. He is the most "genuine" guy I have ever town. I love the man.

In my mind, this picture perfectly captures what Jerry Young is all about. Jerry's old pickup, with his bed set up in the back. Cub hauled on the rear, on a rack he made myself. Jerry would say, "This is all I need to be comfortable, so why complicate things?"

Frank Watson

My association with Jerry Young dates to 1973. I was just a kid and had gone up to the Roaring Branch Motorsports facility just to hang around. This guy came up to me and asked it. I'd like to help him build some "sections." "Sections of what?" I asked as I didn't know a darned thing about observed trials back then. Well, Jerry didn't let that stand in the way of securing some free labor, and before I knew it, I was helping him out on a regular basis, including at the world round in 1978.

As I grew older, my motorcycling interest turned first to moto-cross, then to dirt track racing, and eventually to speedway, at which I managed a considerable level of success. Once my professional racing career concluded, I decided to give trials a try as a rider. I purchased a bike from Ryan Young and got after it. By chance, Jerry happened to come to my house to visit one day. I showed Jerry that I have a good bit of property on which to ride, and the next thing I knew, he was coming over quite regularly to ride with me. Although Jerry was a bit older even then, he still possessed mad skills and wasn't shy about trying to teach me his techniques. He made it look so easy! But I struggled, and at times I could tell Jerry was feeling a bit frustrated at my lack of trials-riding ability. But, hey, I was receiving personal training from Jerry Young! What could be better? It was great fun. We would ride, then sit and drink beer, then ride some more, then drink some more. What a life! More recently, I have been involved with the folks who currently utilize the Roaring Branch property and helped Jerry to secure a permanent home there for his Pennsylvania Trials Riders memorial.

Jerry has been a terrific friend. He is great fan to be around, is an awesome rider, and never, ever ceases promoting the sport of observed trials. Jerry has got to be one of the greatest teachers in the world because it seems there is nothing he enjoys more than encouraging others to experience the fun and excitement of observed trials riding.

Jim "Jimmy Z" Zuroske

I've lived in the Indianapolis, Indiana, area my entire life and began riding just as soon as I was able to save up enough money from delivering newspapers to buy my first motorcycle. It wasn't until 1987, however, that I became involved with observed trials riding. Up to that point, I had dabbled in motocross and dirt track racing, but it wasn't until I discovered trials that I found the form of riding that I really enjoy and have stuck with. Since then, I have been extensively involved with the sport, have ridden events all over the country, and spent a number of years as president of Trials Incorporated.

My association with Jerry began in a most indirect way. A 1988 Beta was my first trials bike. There were no Beta dealers anywhere near the Indianapolis area, but through the *Trials Competition* newspaper (no Internet back then, of course), I found that there was a guy named Jerry Young over in Pennsylvania who was selling Beta motorcycles and parts. What followed were a series of telephone calls during which time I inquired with Jerry regularly for information on parts and service for my Beta, plus bugged him extensively for trials insight in general. I also obtained a copy of Jerry's trials-training video and learned much from his practice techniques. And, of course, along the way, I learned much of who Jerry is and what he has accomplished in the sport as well as all about Ryan and his success in observed trials.

I met Ryan at a national in 1990, but it was not until 2001 that I finally met Jerry in person. We were at the Saddleback East event, and as had been the case with Ryan, I was total starstruck just to be around Jerry. Even though he was older at that time, Jerry was still riding extremely well. From that point on, we began to see each other at various events, more frequently, and I like to think that I had become somewhat of a friend to Jerry. This all led to one of my favorite stories about Jerry, which I like to call "Snake Act One." Jerry and I were both at one of the Ute Cup events, in 2005 I believe. Due to him being a bit older by then, and considering the severity of the Ute Cup, Jerry had stepped down to ride the advanced line while at that point I had advanced to the same line. Learning of this, I excitedly approached Jerry and told him that I was going to "hawk" him all weekend—follow him, copy his lines, and do everything I could to beat him. Jerry's response was just a grin, and he said, "That's great! Maybe we could ride together."

So, off we go, and although Jerry had started a few rows ahead of me, I blitzed the first few sections and managed to catch up to him. With so many riders participating, there would typically be a number of participants waiting to ride each section. And as a result, there was consistently a row of bikes parked before the start of each section, with the riders off and walking their intended lines. I pulled up to the back of such a line of bikes at the next section we came to and leaned my motorcycle against a tree. Jerry, however, rode right on past the line of bikes and pulled up and parked just at the start gate. I jogged over to catch up with him, and we proceeded to walk the section. Jerry was very patient and really took his time walking the section, considering every obstacle. I was quite anxious, wanting to get back on my bike and ride, but I stuck with Jerry, looking at everything as he did, intent on eventually copying his every move.

Once back at my bike, I expected Jerry to wait his turn to ride the section, at which point I would have moved back up next to him and could observe his ride through the section. Instead, and much to my surprise, Jerry was immediately waved on to ride the section by the other riders, a very sportsmanlike gesture, to help an older rider stay on the time schedule. So, there I was, some thirty yards or so back down the trail, straining to watch Jerry ride the section and study his moves. And wouldn't you know it, that old stinker rode an entirely different line than what he had walked, finished the section, and was gone! I never saw him again the rest of the day. The old pro had "ditched" me, gotten rid of the pest who had expressed intent to shadow him, learn from his lines and techniques, and use the lessons learned to beat him. Jerry, you crafty old dog. We had a good laugh about it later, of course, and I can't help but smile every time I think about that day—Jerry teaching me a lesson about "The Snake Line." And note, I call this little story "Snake Act One" because there would be similar lessons by Jerry in the future, demonstrating how to outwit a competitor.

A perfect example of who Jerry is, and what he is all about, comes to mind from my experience camping with him at a national event in Colorado back in 2007. My son and I were riding the entire national circuit that year as Christopher was making his first attempt at earning a national title. Our transporter at the time was an old Chevy Beauville van. Jerry was driving a similar van back then, and I guess we may have considered this mutual choice of simple haulers put us in a somewhat more basic class compared to those folks with much more elaborate rigs. We had arrived at the event and were considering where to set up when Jerry pulled in and asked where we thought it would be best to camp. Looking around, we both decided we wanted to get off somewhere "away from all the generators" and eventually settled in a quiet, somewhat secluded spot. My tremendously supportive wife always brought along plenty of food, and as we prepared for dinner, I asked Jerry what his plans were. He responded that he would probably heat up a can of soup or something, so I invited him to join us. After a hearty meal, Jerry expressed considerable and heartfelt thanks and complimented my wife repeatedly, indicating that, thanks to her, "We ate like kings." You have to know Jerry to understand just how much it means to him to extend such a simple gesture as a shared meal. He is such a basic, down-to-earth, appreciative individual, one who never loses sight of the simplest things in life, such as good friends, good food, and good times.

I've got to comment on Jerry's little Triumph Cub. Much has been said about that bike—how Jerry modified it, worked on it for years, and made the thing good enough to perform exceptionally well in observed trials competition. What really amazes me, in addition to all that Jerry has done with the bike mechanically, is all the various riding he has done with *one* motorcycle. Early on, he and his wife rode the bike on the street and traveled on it. Jerry later used the Cub for trail riding and competed in enduros on it and then, of course, eventually modified it effectively enough to win an observed trials championship. Think about that for a minute, and try to imagine a road-legal bike, ridden thousands of miles on the street, and ridden off-road, and ridden in off-road competition, and eventually winning a National Observed Trials Championship—the very same motorcycle! That is unbelievable! What an accomplishment as well as a testament to Jerry's ingenuity, determination, riding skills, and to an amazing little motorcycle.

As a rider, I consider Jerry Young to be an absolute master of observed trials. He has traveled so much, ridden in so many different events, and learned from so many great riders. In the way he rides, as well as in all aspects of Jerry's life, he is so methodical, always has a plan. And his impact on the sport, Jerry took on every challenge imaginable when hosting his national and international events, and not only persevered, but also did it all right. Really put some spice on his events. He drove everything forward, pushed to make things happen, and in the end, produced some of the best events the observed trials world has ever seen. For those efforts, as well as virtually everything he has accomplished in his life, I have a tremendous amount of respect for Jerry.

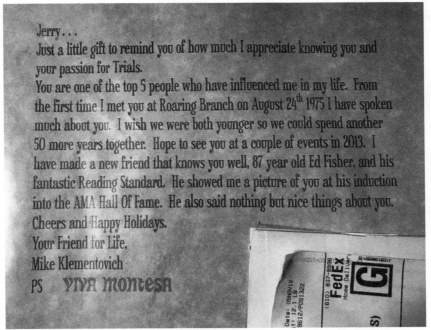

Jerry...

Just a little gift to remind you of how much I appreciate knowing you and your passion for Trials.

You are one of the top 5 people who have influenced me in my life. From the first time I met you at Roaring Branch on August 24th 1975 I have spoken much about you. I wish we were both younger so we could spend another 50 more years together. Hope to see you at a couple of events in 2013. I have made a new friend that knows you well, 87 year old Ed Fisher, and his fantastic Reading Standard. He showed me a picture of you at his induction into the AMA Hall Of Fame. He also said nothing but nice things about you. Cheers and Happy Holidays.

Your Friend for Life,

Mike Klementovich

PS   VIVA MONTESA

I was completely overwhelmed by these gracious comments from family and friends. We had solicited for a few comments from folks to help provide perspective on my story, but I never expected to receive such a favorable response. Looking back on my life, I wish above all, that I have had a positive influence on other's lives. This note from an old friend, Mike Klementovich, provides some hope that I have indeed done so.

CHAPTER 14
Trials Today

My Take on What the Sport Has Evolved Into

It is great fun to bring the Cub out and mix it up with much newer bikes and much younger riders. We never fail to impress with both the Cub's and my(!) abilities. Such somber faces on everyone in this picture. We're listening to the rider's meeting, and apparently are all taking it quite seriously.

In wrapping up this book, I can't help but comment on what I think about the sport as it currently exists. I'm not going to spend a lot of time on this, and I sure don't want to take anything away from modern equipment or today's riders. The bikes are amazing. So far beyond what my little Cub is, it's hard to believe. And the riders? True athletes, demonstrating amazing skills and tremendous talent.

So, trials riders today may ask, what's this old guy know about modern observed trials?

It has been my great pleasure to have rubbed elbows over the years with many of the greatest riders in the sport. Here I am with one of the young stars—Quinn Wentzel.

Well, let me tell you. Many things have changed over the years, but the essence of the sport has not. Observed trials was, is, and will continue to be the same challenge. It's man and machine against the terrain. Simple as that. So, here's my take. And, again, this is not intended to take anything away from current riders, clubs which host events, or anyone else involved in the sport because at the heart of it, observed trials is a great aspect of motorcycling, which enables participation by a multitude of riders with varying levels of skill.

And yet bottom line, at the national level anyway, trials has taken a very different path from its origins. There are so many lines and so many classes, the waters are all muddied. And about "the gate" system, for example, riders must be able to read cards as they ride then chose what path to take. It's easy to get lost in a section! Plus, the bikes are so good, skilled riders are zeroing everything. It's all too predictable. And much of this has to do with the conditions. Amazingly skilled riders are pulling off incredible, truly impressive moves. And yet much of this action takes place in quite favorable conditions, with plenty of traction and wild yet predictable obstacles.

Before I come off as an old guy who doesn't know what he's talking about, permit me to toot my own horn a bit. Remember that fellow I talked about earlier in the book who put on hundreds of local trials events and multiple national and international trials events and who has traveled all over the country and even overseas to compete? Well, that was me! So yes, I *do* know what I am talking about.

I am very happy to have always done my part as an ambassador, and continual promoter, of the sport of Observed Trials. I never stop reaching out to people from all aspects of motorcycling, such as the legendary John Penton, whom I am proud to have provided an autographed number plate.

It may sound as if I think the trials events I put on back home here in Pennsylvania were just the cat's ass. Well, you know what? They were! We had everything that observed trials competition is supposed to confront riders with—mud, water, rocks, logs, off-cambers, slippery conditions, and so on. These are the *real* obstacles, which take away points and provide riders with genuine, unpredictable challenges. Natural terrain, which features just these types of obstacles, are what trials is supposed to be all about. However, such conditions simply do not exist everywhere or just anywhere. My early experiences out in California demonstrated that. The promoters made a valiant effort, but they just didn't have the appropriate terrain to work with.

Young people are the key to continuation of our sport. Observed Trials is very fortunate to have new, young riders coming on board all the time. Just as important, are folks who, like me, work behind the scenes to promote and market trials. One such individual is the young lady here—Stephanie Vetterly, who is not only an accomplished rider, but also a journalist, who works tirelessly to photograph and chronicle Trials and other off-road events, all shared through modern media.

And yet trials competition takes place all over the US, including the national events. And in those events where the riders are dealing with amazing yet conquerable, predictable obstacles, which they often clean, their skills and capabilities are somewhat limited. And the result, US riders are not on par with the Europeans, who frequently are dealing with the basic, natural obstacles of mud, water, and the like.

Fortunately, the sport of observed trials in the United States is doing quite well. We've always been a niche facet of motorcycle competition but have maintained a solid core of dedicated clubs, promoters, and riders. Throughout my involvement with the sport, right from the very beginning, I did everything I could to make the sport better. I participated, hosted events, sold the bikes and gear, put on demos and riding schools—did everything I could to promote trials. And for what purpose? Why, to share the fun, of course. And at its core, that's what observed trials is all about. It's a motorcycle activity which does not require a huge investment in purchase or maintenance of equipment, does not tear up the equipment, and is a relatively safe sport, providing an avenue for people of all ages to participate, have fun, and enjoy competition with low potential for injury. Trials requires a relatively small amount of property, is quiet, doesn't tear up the land, and is spectator-friendly.

I am very proud of the role I've played in the support, growth, and promotion of the sport of Observed Trials. And, along the way I have evidently become pretty good at riding, too. Plus, this picture shows that I've never lost my interest in the sport, pleasure in riding, and desire to win. I've always enjoyed it all, and always will.

These certainly are the traits we have always used to promote our sport, and they are still valid today. Observed trials has been my favorite form of motorcycling since I first began riding. It's provided me a lifetime's worth of fun, adventure, excitement, and travel and introduced me to many, many wonderful friends and associates over the years. I have greatly enjoyed every minute of it and wouldn't trade my experiences for anything. It's been a great life up on the pegs.

The End

I could never thank my wife, Kelly enough, for her unending support and encouragement. Early on, she and I promised each other that we would never stand in the way of either of our interests or pursuits. It's always worked out fine, and as a result, we each have memories of many wonderful experiences and adventures.

About the Author

From his humble beginnings in Williamsport, Pennsylvania, to founding of the Pennsylvania Trials Riders Association, to earning America's first AMA National Observed Trials Championship on a Triumph Tiger Cub, followed by a lifetime of motorcycling adventures, activities, and pursuits, as well as many, many additional, amazing experiences, Jerry Young has seen more, done more, and lived more than many people ever will. This is his story.

CPSIA information can be obtained
at www.ICGtesting.com
Printed in the USA
BVHW021801161121
621783BV00020B/463